Putting it up with Honey

Putting it up with Honey

a natural foods canning and preserving cookbook

by Susan Geiskopf

illustrated by Linda Cleaver

Quicksilver Productions
Post Office Box 340
Ashland, Oregon 97520

Library of Congress Cataloging in Publication Data

Geiskopf, Susan, 1950–
    Putting it up with Honey.

    Includes index.
    1. Canning and preserving. 2. Cookery (Honey)
3. Cookery (Natural foods) I. Title.
TX601.G36   641.4'2   78-59871
ISBN 0-930356-13-6

3   4   5   6   7   8   9   84   83   82   81   80

INTERNATIONAL STANDARD BOOK NUMBER: 0-930356-13-6

LIBRARY OF CONGRESS CATALOG CARD NUMBER: 78-59871

Published and distributed in the United States
and Internationally by Quicksilver Productions

With thanks to:

Guy Hadler for growing so many delicious fruits and vegetables.
Carole Fletcher for helping me test so many recipes over that hot summer stove.
Mindy Lackey Toomay for all of the long hours of editing and taking care of goofs.
and all those other people for encouraging this endeavor.

Contents

Introduction

It's All in the Jar

It's All in the Jar

Canning with honey? Yes, you can *can with honey!* Honey is one of nature's oldest preservatives and one of the first sweeteners known.

Putting it Up with Honey is a book about food preservation with recipes which use no sugar. Pure natural honey tastes good, contains traces of minerals, vitamins and enzymes and assimilates in such a way as to maintain a fairly constant blood sugar balance.

Honey is made up primarily of glucose and fructose. Glucose enters the bloodstream rapidly but fructose is assimilated over a four-hour time span. Refined white sugar, traditionally used in canning, is almost pure sucrose. Sucrose is the most rapidly assimilated kind of sugar. Its intake drastically increases the blood sugar level. In an emergency reaction hormones are released: the endocrine "islets" of the pancreas work to restore the blood sugar balance by producing lots of insulin fast. So much insulin is produced so fast that the blood sugar level dips too low—sometimes dangerously low. This blood sugar starvation then causes a sugar craving. In addition, the appetite, confused by sugar, desires less proteins and fats necessary for proper metabolism.

The recipes in **Putting it Up with Honey** have been tested for nutrition, taste and appearance. They present an excellent method of preserving foods to retain their maximum nutritional value, to taste fresh and sweet, and to look delicious.

Spending an afternoon with a friend putting up a lug of peaches makes the process easier and promises a pantry of summer's bounty on the coldest winter day.

Chapter 1

The Hows and Whys of Canning

The Hows and Whys of Canning

The principles of food preservation must be clearly understood in order to produce a product that is safe to eat and appealing to the palate. With the exceptions of some fruits and a few vegetables, fresh foods must be eaten soon after harvesting or they begin to spoil— to change color and flavor and, finally, to decompose. Storage in the refrigerator will delay these processes, but special preparation is needed to halt them completely. Successful canning requires that specially prepared foods be locked into a sterile container where the agents that promote decay cannot survive. Heating destroys the troublesome organisms and the sealed containers prevent re-contamination of the preserved foods. The acid content naturally occurring in foods, the pH factor, determines to a great extent the spoilage microorganisms a food can host. You need not worry about spoilage if you adhere to the time, temperature, and technique most appropriate for the acid content of the food you are canning. The techniques presented here assure good results and de-mystify the threats of spoilage and botulism. The guidelines will show you how to detect spoilage, should it occur.

Canning with honey

Honey has been recognized as a superior source of usable sugars. It enhances the fresh flavor of canned foods as well as helping to retain the food's natural color (though honey tends to create a somewhat darker product).

A typical sampling of honey contains 41% levulose (fructose—the most common sugar occurring in fruits), 34% dextrose (glucose—the type of sugar found in blood), 17% moisture, and 8% other complex sugar types, acids, amino acids (proteins), trace minerals and vitamins. Honey contains the enzyme "inhibine", which prevents honey from molding; as it ages, it merely crystallizes. To maintain honey's maximum nutritional value, you may wish to process food without it, adding it to sweeten the product just before it is eaten.

The standard cup measure is 8 oz., based on the weight of water. One cup of sugar, however, weighs only 7 oz.; a cup of honey weighs 12 oz. The standard cup of honey provides 9½ oz. of sweetener, so when converting sugar recipes, remember that only ¾ cup of honey, or less, according to taste, is needed to replace a full cup of sugar. Also, cut down on the amount of liquid required in the original recipe or cook the fruit down a bit to compensate for the honey's extra moisture. Remember to use a large, high-walled kettle when cooking food with honey, as it tends to foam.

Containers and lids

The techniques discussed in this book will require the use of glass jars and metal sealing lids and rings. Glass canning jars, known as "mason jars" for their nineteenth-century American inventor, John L. Mason, are the standard jars used in home canning. These reusable jars are available in a variety of sizes and shapes. They are suitable for home canning and home freezing. The glass in these jars is tempered to withstand either the heat and pressure of a pressure canner or the below-zero cold of a freezer. In addition, the jars have a threaded mouth so that a flat metal lid with a screw band makes an air-tight closure.

To use the flat metal lids, place the lid on the rim of the jar with the sealing edge next to the glass. Screw the band firmly to hold the lid in place. Do not loosen the ring until the jar is sealed and cooled. During processing, air is exhausted from the jar; as the jar cools a vacuum pulls the lid tight. Flat lids are designed for one-time usage. The screw bands may be re-used as long as they are not bent out of shape or rusty. All jars can be sterilized and reused if they are not cracked or chipped. A damaged jar might not seal properly and could explode.

Canning Methods

The **raw pack** method is used for low-density foods, such as tomatoes, peaches and pears, which will hold their shape better when packed raw. Pack the jars firmly with the food. If additional liquid is required, use boiling water or hot syrup. Since jars of raw pack foods are cold, processing must begin in hot water which is **gradually** brought to the boiling point so the jars won't crack. The processing time is usually longer for raw pack foods. Exact time required in the boiling-water bath is given with each recipe.

The **hot pack** method is used to introduce new flavors by adding spices to the produce and to permit a more solid pack. Foods differ in the amount of pre-heating or cooking they require. Exact times are given with each recipe. These foods require less processing time in a boiling-water bath than do raw pack foods because they are thoroughly hot beforehand.

Allow adequate headroom in the jars for both the raw pack and the hot pack methods. Headroom is the space between the top of the food and the bottom of the lid. Headroom allows solid foods room to expand and allows room for liquids to bubble up during processing. The amount of necessary headroom varies slightly and is stipulated in each recipe. If there is inadequate headroom, some of the contents may be forced out with the air, leaving a deposit on the sealing surface and ruining the seal. Too much headroom may cause the food on the top to discolor and may also prevent a good seal because the processing time might not be long enough to exhaust the excess air.

Food processing techniques

In the **open kettle method,** sterilized hot jars are filled with boiling foods. Sterilized seals are put on immediately so that as the jars cool the steam from the contents condenses creating a vacuum which completes the seal. This exclusion of air is vital to the preservation of food because air carries living organisms which cause spoilage. Only high-acid foods, those having a high natural sugar content or foods that have been vinegared, may be canned by this traditional method. Although many long-time canners still use the open-kettle method, I do not use nor recommend it because it does not safeguard against possible contamination by airborne organisms during the transfer from kettle to jar.

The **hot-water bath** is the method which merely pasteurizes the food and the containers rather than processing them, since it does not maintain a real boil but simmers at 180° F/

82°C to 190°F/88°C. This temperature sterilizes the jars, not the food. Jars are sterilized in a hot-water bath before being filled and a boiling-water bath is then required to process the food. The hot-water bath method may be used for sweet fruit juices.

The **boiling-water bath** processes foods at 212°F/100°C, at which temperature bacteria, yeast, and molds cannot survive. This technique forces air from the containers, thus insuring perfect seals. Processing time varies for different foods, altitudes, container sizes, and atmospheric conditions.

A boiling-water bath is achieved simply by filling a large canning kettle about half way with hot tap water and heating to boiling. Place clean jars in the kettle to sterilize as the water is heating. Scald the lids by putting them in boiling water which has been removed from the flame and keep them there until ready for use. Prepare the food which is to be processed as indicated in the recipe. Spoon the hot food into the hot jars. Release any air bubbles by running a knife or spatula down between the food and the jar, but do not stir, as this may create air pockets. Wipe the sealing edge of the jar clean with a sterilized towel. Place a lid on each jar and screw down tightly. The jars should be held in place with a canning rack, then lowered into the water bath. Add hot water, if necessary, to bring the water level to about one inch above the tops of the jars. Place a cover on the kettle and count processing time from the moment the water begins a hard boil. Process for the time stipulated in each recipe. Remove the jars carefully in an upright position as tipping sideways or upside down could break the seal. Place the jars on a wire rack or folded towel to cool. This will prevent breaking caused by an abrupt change in surface temperature.

The **pressure canning method** allows the contents of the jars to reach temperatures of 228°F/109°C to 250°F/121°C. This method destroys the tough bacteria present in low-acid foods such as vegetables, meats, and dairy products. Pressure canning is also the best method for soups and major canning projects involving a winter's supply of vegetables. It is not necessary or advisable for high-acid foods, such as fruits, as temperatures above 212°F injure their delicate colors and flavors.

Storage of canned foods

Storage is an important consideration in the canning process. Before storing your canned goods, test the seals on all jars when they are thoroughly cooled. You may hear loud snaps while the jars are cooling. This sound occurs when the vacuum in the jar suddenly pulls down the metal lid to make an air-tight seal. However, sealing is not always accompanied by a loud noise. It may occur as you press the center of a lid on a cooled jar. If the dip in the lid holds, the jar is sealed.

When the seal is good, the metal ring may be removed before storage. If a ring sticks, covering it for a moment with a hot, damp cloth may help loosen it. Wash bands and store in a dry place for reuse if they are not dented, bent, or rusted. Wipe the containers clean before storing and label them to show the contents, date, and the lot number if more than one batch was canned in a day.

It is best to store jars in a cool, dry, dark place. Avoid freezing temperatures or bright sunlight. Either extreme will cause oxidation and loss of color. Foods should be used from year to year, but will keep longer under proper conditions.

Don't use canned foods that show even the slightest sign of spoilage. Look closely at each container before opening it. Bulging jar lids or rings, or a leak, means the seal has broken and the food is spoiled. When you open a container, look for other signs such as spurting liquid, mold, or an off-odor (the smell of a canned product should be pleasant and characteristic of the produce used). If there is any indication of spoilage, do not eat or even taste the contents. Dispose of them so that they cannot be eaten by humans or animals. After emptying a jar of spoiled food, wash the jar in hot, soapy water and rinse; then boil the jar in clean water for 15 minutes. Jars can be re-used as long as they are free of cracks or nicks.

Spoilage organisms

Enzymes are naturally occurring substances in plant and animal tissue which help to promote the organic changes occurring during growth. Enzyme action is present in all raw fruits and vegetables. This is not harmful, but it eventually causes decomposition and changes the flavor, texture and color of the food, making it unappetizing. The decomposition action is slow in cold temperatures, occurs rapidly around 85°F/30°C to 120°F/49°C, and begins to be checked again around 140°F/60°C. Therefore, processing in a boiling-water bath at 212°F prevents enzyme decomposition.

Molds are micro-organisms which occur naturally in soil, air and water. They are microscopic fungi whose dry spores settle on food and start growing. Their threads take the shape of tightly woven fuzz. Some molds, such as certain cheese or bread molds, are valued for their flavors. Others are unpleasant, making the food musty and distasteful. Although they remain alive, molds do not grow below freezing, 32°F/0°C. They grow rapidly between 50°F/10°C to 100°F/38°C. Though their growth slows down at 120°F/49°C, the temperature must reach 190°F/88°C before they are destroyed. When using a hot pack method, remember that the food must still be processed in a boiling-water bath to kill any airborne mold which might contaminate food before the jar is sealed.

Yeasts are fungi grown from the spores that cause fermentation. This action is necessary in hard cider, beer, vinegar, or sauerkraut but is distasteful in fruits or jam. Yeasts are inactive in cold or freezing temperatures but grow rapidly between 50°F/10°C to 100°F/38°C. They are destroyed at 140°F/60°C to 190°F/88°C. Again, the boiling-water bath temperature of 212°F checks this action. Process sealed jars for the stipulated time in a boiling-water bath to stop the growth of spores which settle on cooked food or on the sterilized jars.

Bacteria are present in soil, air and water. They are disease-causing and are tougher than yeasts or molds. Bacteria which may promote food spoilage fall into three categories: genus salmonella, genus staphylococcus aureus, and clostridium botulinum. They can occur only in low-acid foods. Botulin toxins are produced by spores which grow rapidly in the absence of air. They are inactive when frozen, yet survive. Bacteria can be destroyed by canning foods at 240° to 250°F. This temperature, 28° higher than that of a boiling-water bath, can only be reached in a pressure canner. Therefore, you need not fear botulism poisoning if you use the correct method for the particular food you are canning. Before eating any canned low-acid foods, boiling for 15-20 minutes is advised. Contamination by these bacteria is not a hazard with high-acid foods, such as those discussed in this book.

APPROXIMATE POSITION OF
VARIOUS FOOD PRODUCTS ON pH SCALE

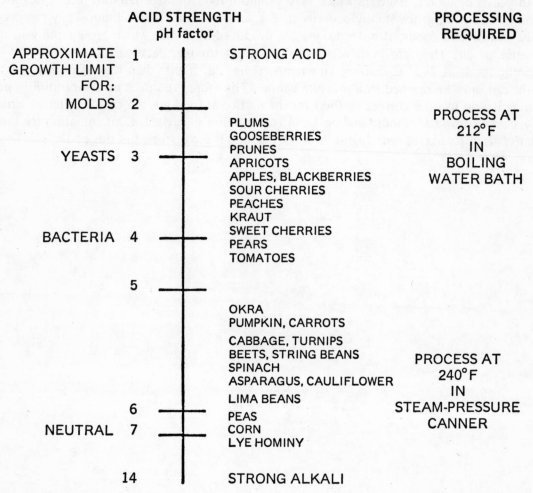

	ACID STRENGTH pH factor		PROCESSING REQUIRED
APPROXIMATE GROWTH LIMIT FOR:	1	STRONG ACID	
MOLDS	2		PROCESS AT 212°F
		PLUMS GOOSEBERRIES	
YEASTS	3	PRUNES APRICOTS APPLES, BLACKBERRIES SOUR CHERRIES PEACHES KRAUT	IN BOILING WATER BATH
BACTERIA	4	SWEET CHERRIES PEARS TOMATOES	
	5		
		OKRA PUMPKIN, CARROTS CABBAGE, TURNIPS BEETS, STRING BEANS SPINACH ASPARAGUS, CAULIFLOWER LIMA BEANS	PROCESS AT 240°F IN STEAM-PRESSURE CANNER
	6	PEAS	
NEUTRAL	7	CORN LYE HOMINY	
	14	STRONG ALKALI	

Temperature of Food for Control of Bacteria

°F	°C	
250	121	Canning temperatures for low-acid vegetables, meat, and poultry in pressure canning.
240	116	
212	100	Canning temperatures for fruits, tomatoes, and pickles in water-bath container.
165	74	Cooking temperatures destroy most bacteria. Time required to kill bacteria decreases as temperature is increased.
140	60	Warming temperatures prevent growth but allow survival of some bacteria.
120	49	Some bacteria growth may occur. Many bacteria survive.
60	15	DANGER ZONE. Temperatures in this zone allow rapid growth of bacteria and production of toxins by some bacteria.
40	4.5	Some growth of food poisoning bacteria may occur. (Do not store meats, poultry, or seafoods for more than a week in the refrigerator.)
32	0	Cold temperatures permit slow growth of some bacteria that cause spoilage.
0	-18	Freezing temperatures stop growth of bacteria, but may allow bacteria to survive. (Do not store food above 10°F for more than a few weeks.)

Helpful Hints

1. Jars must be free of nicks or cracks. Use mason jars to fit the standard seals available. Mason lids screw down rather than being held in place with bails and rubber seals like the old style wire-clamp jars. The metal lid for a mason jar has a rubber ring attached which meets the rim of the jar and creates a seal.

2. Always screw the seal down with a metal band to hold it firmly in place. The band must be firmly tight upon entering the water bath.

3. Do not readjust the band after the jar has been removed from the water bath; this may break the seal.

4. After the jar has cooled for at least 12 hours, if the flat dome lid is firmly sealed to the jar, the band may be removed and reused on another jar.

5. Never re-use a flat dome lid; it will not seal perfectly.

6. Wash and sterilize jars before each use. Keep them warm until used. Do not boil the seals; it may ruin the rubber sealing edge. Place them in water which has been boiled and is still hot.

7. Do not put cold jars of food into a boiling-water bath; they might break.

8. Do not add cold water to a hot canner full of hot jars; always add warm or hot water.

9. Do not knock filled jars against each other.

10. Unload the jars carefully. Set them on a rack or wooden surface to cool. Avoid drafts.

11. Any empty jars, such as mayonnaise jars, may be used for canning as long as they will fit a standard-size canning lid. Avoid packing pickled foods in them, however, because the residue of oil left inside the jar might react with the pickles and turn them soft or add an undesirable flavor. Whole tomatoes should be canned in standard mason jars, because tomatoes can crack jars during processing.

12. Jars of more dense food products tend to take longer to seal completely after removal from the canning kettle. Do not be alarmed if you don't hear the "pop" of the seal immediately after removing the jar from the canner—it can take 30 minutes or longer.

13. Load the filled jars into the canning kettle rack working from side to side, counter-balancing the weight so the rack won't tip over. Follow a similar procedure when unloading the canner.

14. The food in jars that do not seal may be re-heated and spooned into hot sterilized jars and reprocessed.

15. Always wash jars and put them in a hot water bath to sterilize before you begin to prepare the food. The jars will be ready when you need them.

Metric Conversion Table

To Change	To	Multiply By
ounces (oz.)	grams (g)	28
pounds (lbs.)	kilograms (kg)	0.45
teaspoons (tsp.)	milliliters (ml)	5
tablespoons (tbl.)	milliliters (ml)	15
fluid ounces (oz.)	milliliters (ml)	30
cups (c.)	liters (l)	0.24
pints (pt.)	liters (l)	0.47
quarts (qt.)	liters (l)	0.95
gallons (gal.)	liters (l)	3.8
temperature ($°F$)	temperature ($°C$)	5/9 after subtracting 32

9$°F$ above boiling equals 5$°C$ above boiling.

Measures

Dash	less than ⅛ teaspoon
3 teaspoons	1 tablespoon (½ fluid ounce)
2 tablespoons	⅛ cup (1 fluid ounce)
4 tablespoons	¼ cup (2 fluid ounces)
5⅓ tablespoons	⅓ cup (2⅔ fluid ounces)
8 tablespoons	½ cup (4 fluid ounces)
10⅔ tablespoons	⅔ cup (5⅓ fluid ounces)
12 tablespoons	¾ cup (6 fluid ounces)
14 tablespoons	⅞ cup (7 fluid ounces)
16 tablespoons	1 cup
1 gill	½ cup
1 cup	8 fluid ounces
2 cups	1 pint
2 pints	1 quart (approx. 1 liter)
4 quarts	1 gallon
8 quarts	1 peck
4 pecks	1 bushel
1 gram	0.035 ounces
1 ounce	28.35 grams
16 ounces	1 pound (453.59 grams)
1 kilogram	2.21 pounds

Water-bath canner

Jars, seals and rings

Colander for draining

Wide-mouth funnel

Wooden spoons, long-handled

6- to 8-quart enameled kettle for pickles

Jar lifter

Long-handled slotted spoon

Wire basket for blanching

Ladle

Tongs

6- to 8-quart stainless steel
or enameled kettle for pre-cooking foods

Food thermometer— pencil-
shaped glass types are best

Pot holders, dish cloths and towels

Jelly bag

Racks for cooling jars

Sieve or strainer for pureeing

Labels

Heat pad

Chapter 2

Jams, Preserves, Butters and Conserves

Jams, Preserves, Butters and Conserves

The secret to a good jam, preserve, butter or conserve is in the correct ratio of fruit and honey. For best results these spreads should be prepared in small batches so that the temperature can be better controlled. The honey should be a light variety, such as clover. Darker honeys tend to have a strong flavor of their own which will mask the fruit flavor. Distinct flavors may be achieved by adding spices or extracts which compliment the orchard-fresh fruits. Honey preserves have a delicious fruit flavor rather than the heavy sugar-sweet taste characteristic of most sugar preserves.

Jams & Jellies

Jams are made by cooking crushed or chopped fruit with honey in a high-walled pan, providing sufficient room for a good rolling boil. Keep this point in mind when using honey as it tends to froth more than sugar. To make a good firm jam always prepare it in small batches. The mixture should be cooked rapidly to obtain the desired consistency and stirred often to prevent scorching. After the honey dissolves, the mixture should reach $8°F/4½°C$ above the boiling point of water to gel. The individual recipes give specific times and temperatures. Use a candy thermometer to measure temperatures accurately and check the boiling point of water on the day you are canning because it may vary a few degrees depending on atmospheric conditions or altitude.

Jam may be tested for firmness (the gel point) by scooping some out with a metal spoon to see if it rounds-up into drops as it is poured. You might also quick-cool some jam by placing some on a saucer in the freezer for a couple of minutes. If the substance becomes somewhat firm, the jam is ready to be put up. The correct temperature and the ratio of fruit to honey are the keys to obtaining a firm consistency.

Jelly is the gelled juice without pieces of fruit. It should be clear and firm yet tender. Jelly making isn't much different from making jam except that a jelly bag will be needed. A jelly bag holds the fruit allowing the juice to drain. Commercial bags, which can be found at most department stores or hardware stores, come with a metal stand from which they can be suspended. However, a bag can be made from several thicknesses of closely woven cheese-cloth, of unbleached muslin, or canton flannel with the napped side in. The corners would then be tied together and suspended by a cord. Be sure to wash the fabric before using.

When the jelly has cooked for the time specified in the recipe, test for the gel point. The liquid should round-up into drops as you begin to roll it off the spoon. If the drops come together as a sheet as it falls, the jelly is done. If a sheet does not form, cook longer and test again.

This gel test is widely used, but is not always completely dependable.

Preserves

Preserves are made by cooking large pieces of fruit in a light to heavy syrup. The fruit maintains its shape while becoming tender. Preserves should be cooked in a wide, deep pan. The mixture is slowly heated to a boil then cooked rapidly until the fruit becomes tender, suspended in a very thick syrup. The syrup may be made from pure date sugar instead of honey for a flavor variation.

Butters

Butters are made from fruit pulp which has been pressed through a sieve or colander to produce a fine texture. The pulp is then cooked down with a small amount of honey and made fragrant with a measure of sweet spices. Since butters use only half as much honey as most jams, jellies or conserves, the fruit flavor is even more pronounced than in the sweeter spreads.

Butters should be cooked uncovered, to give the water time to evaporate and to allow the fruit mixture to thicken. Cooking time depends on the size of the saucepan and the heat used. As it goes "glub-glub" toward the end of the cooking time it should be stirred constantly to prevent scorching. To test doneness, spoon a bit of the fruit butter onto a cold saucer. If no liquid separates from the butter, it is ready.

Conserves & Marmalades

Conserves are a combination of fruits, nuts, honey, and raisins. The fruit, honey, and raisins are cooked like jam and the consistency should be similar to that of jam. Always add the nuts during the last 5 minutes of cooking time, stirring often to prevent scorching.

Marmalades differ from a conserve in that they contain small pieces of fruit or citrus peel suspended in a transparent gel. Part of the white rind should be included because it contains most of the pectin.

Pectin and Agar-Agar

The thickening process may be hastened by the addition of either agar-agar or fruit pectins. Agar-agar is a seaweed derivative which thickens like gelatin. This substance absorbs moisture rapidly and retains it as well as being easily digestible and flavorless. Agar-agar is available in stick, powder, or flake form and may be readily found in Asian food stores or natural food stores. The basic proportions for using agar-agar are as follows:

1½ tablespoons agar-agar powder will gel 8 cups fruit
3 tablespoons agar-agar flakes will gel 8 cups fruit
2½ sticks agar-agar will gel 9 cups fruit
1 tablespoon agar-agar powder will gel 3½ cups liquid
2 tablespoons agar-agar flakes will gel 3½ cups liquid
1 stick agar-agar will gel 3 cups liquid.

Pectin is another substance which causes fruits to gel. It is made from tart apples or other high-acid fruits, such as currants. Recipes for two natural fruit pectins, which may be prepared in season and canned for future use, are contained in the recipe section of this chapter. Commercial pectins are also available and can be used in these recipes, but be sure to read the label and check for any undesirable additives.

Testing Fruit for Pectin Content

Mix: 1½ teaspoons honey
1 tablespoon Epsom salts
2 tablespoons cooked fruit juice

Stir well and let stand for 20 minutes. If the mixture forms into a semi-solid mass the juice contains sufficient pectin. It is not necessary to taste the mixture.

Testing Fruit for Acid Content

Juice high in pectin may lack necessary acid to make a good jam or jelly. The fruit should be as tart as a mixture of:

1 teaspoon lemon juice
3 tablespoons water

Taste this mixture, then taste the fruit juice or crushed fruit.
Lemon juice may be added to increase tartness.

Processing Jams, Preserves, Butters and Conserves

All jams, preserves, butters, and conserves are spooned hot into hot sterilized jars, filled to within one-quarter inch of the top. The jars are then processed in a boiling-water bath for 10 minutes. The water level should be at least one inch over the tops of the jars and the water must be hot when the jars are lowered in. Start counting processing time as soon as the water in the canner reaches a good rolling boil. The canner should have a lid; this helps keep the water at a rolling boil. This final processing insures that all airborne bacteria and fungi are destroyed.

After processing the jars, remove them carefully and stand them on a rack or towel away from drafts. Cool for about 12 hours. Then test the seals by pressing the lids down with your finger. If they stay down, they're sealed. Store in a cool, dry, dark place.

The jams, preserves, butters, and conserves are now ready for your morning toast or afternoon tarts. They're also tasty over whole wheat waffles or pancakes. Delicious desserts can be made using your preserves as cake filler, as ice cream and yogurt topping, or as pie filling. A bedtime treat can be made by simply spreading jam on crisp-bread or crackers. Eat and enjoy!

Helpful Hints

1. Cook the fruit substance until it begins to thicken before adding the honey. Honey dissolves rapidly and therefore does not require a long cooking time.

2. Cranberries, quinces, green apples, crab apples, blackberries, concord grapes, plums, gooseberries, and orange and lemon rind contain pectin and acid, both of which are necessary to make the product gel. Peaches, pears, cherries, strawberries, pineapples, and rhubarb contain practically no pectin when ripe, so pectin or some other gelling substance must be added. Pears and sweet apples, although high in pectin, contain practically no acid and so require the addition of lemon juice.

3. Boil jams, conserves, marmalades, and preserves until the temperature is 9°F/5°C above the boiling point of water. This yields a firm product.

4. Wring out a jelly bag with warm water before squeezing fruit through it. This avoids absorption of juice by the cloth.

5. Squeezing the jelly bag will yield more juice but give a cloudy product. If you choose to squeeze the bag, you might try filtering the juice a second time.

6. After each use, scrupulously clean the jelly bag before storing; any remaining juice or pulp will sour.

7. Always spoon off any foam which forms while cooking before you pour the mixture into the jars.

8. Remember to wipe the rims with a **clean,** damp cloth to remove any spilled food which could prevent the jar from sealing.

9. Berries contain more water in proportion to their weight than do larger fruits or vegetables. It is best to pre-cook the berries so they will not float to the top of the jar when making preserves.

10. Scorching is a problem when making jam. Using a copper-bottomed pan or a white enameled pan with an aluminum heat pad reduces the chance of scorching.

11. If the product should scorch while cooking, immediately remove the substance from the pot and finish cooking in a clean container. To clean the bottom of the scorched pot, sprinkle baking soda over the burned area and add a couple of inches of water. Simmer for a few minutes, then remove from heat and cool a bit. Wipe the scorched food from the pot; no scraping will be necessary.

Altitude, Temperature and the Gel Point

		F	C			F	C
Sea level	boil to	222°	105.5°	7,500 ft.	boil to	207°	97°
2,000 ft.	boil to	217°	103°	10,000 ft.	boil to	203°	95°
5,000 ft.	boil to	212°	100°	15,000 ft.	boil to	193°	89°

At higher altitudes the boiling point of water decreases and processing times must be increased. At altitudes less than 1,000 feet above sea level, the processing times given are sufficient. At higher altitudes processing times should be increased as follows:

Altitude	If recipe calls for 20 minutes or less increase time by:	If recipe calls for more than 20 minutes increase time by:
1,000 feet	1 minute	2 minutes
2,000 feet	2 minutes	4 minutes
3,000 feet	3 minutes	6 minutes
4,000 feet	4 minutes	8 minutes
5,000 feet	5 minutes	10 minutes
6,000 feet	6 minutes	12 minutes
7,000 feet	7 minutes	14 minutes
8,000 feet	8 minutes	16 minutes
9,000 feet	9 minutes	18 minutes
10,000 feet	10 minutes	20 minutes

Apple Pectin

Yield: 4 half-pints

7 large apples (tart)
4 cups water
2 tablespoons lemon juice

Wash apples and cut into small pieces without peeling. Add the water and the lemon juice. Boil for 40 minutes. Press through a jelly bag, then strain juice through a flannel bag. Be sure to wet both bags with warm water before squeezing the juice through, so the bags won't absorb much juice. Boil the juice rapidly for 15 minutes. Pour boiling juice into sterilized jars and seal. Process 5 minutes in a boiling-water bath.

Use for fruits which lack pectin, such as peaches, pears, cherries, strawberries, pineapples, and rhubarb. Add 1 cup of fruit pectin for each cup of fruit.

Red Currant Pectin

Wash the currants and stew them gently in enough water to cover. Cook until soft. Mash and place them in a jelly bag and allow to drip into a bowl overnight. Do not squeeze the bag. Also, be sure to dampen the bag with warm water so it will not absorb so much juice. Pour the collected juice into sterilized ½-pint jars. Seal. Process 5 minutes in boiling-water bath.

Use 1 cup of currant pectin for each cup of fruit.

(Especially good when mixed with raspberries or strawberries.)

Extracting Lemon Juice

Put the lemons in hot water for a few minutes before cutting or squeezing them. This results in more juice being extracted.

Apricot Jam

Yield: 6 half-pints

6 cups apricots
2½ cups honey
¼ cup lemon juice
1 box powdered pectin

Wash and cut apricots and put them in a large kettle. Mash them and heat slowly. As the juice begins to run, the heat can be increased. Cook the apricots for about 15 minutes. Add the pectin; stir in well. Bring to a boil and add the honey and lemon. Stir well. Heat rapidly to a full rolling boil, 9°F/5°C above boiling, and cook for 5 minutes. Spoon hot mixture into jars to within ½-inch of top. Complete seals. Process in a boiling-water bath for 10 minutes.

Apricot-Date Jam

Yield: 6 half-pints

6 cups apricots
2 cups date sugar
¼ cup lemon juice
1 box powdered pectin

Wash and cut apricots. Mash them in a large kettle. Add the pectin; stir well. Bring to a boil and add the date sugar and lemon. Bring to 9°F/5°C above boiling and cook for 10 minutes. Spoon hot jam into hot sterilized jars, to within ¼-inch of top. Complete seals. Process in a boiling-water bath for 15 minutes.

This jam makes an excellent filling for a linzertorte.

Amber-Apricot Jam

Yield: 4 half-pints

½ pound dried apricots
rind of one lemon, grated
¼ cup grated carrot
2½ cups water
2½ cups honey
⅓ cup lemon juice

Combine apricots, lemon rind, carrots, and water. Cover and place over low heat. Bring to a boil slowly, stirring often. Cook gently for 30 minutes. Add honey and lemon juice and cook for 30 minutes more. Stir frequently as the jam thickens. Spoon into hot sterilized jars to within ½-inch of top. Complete seals. Process in a boiling-water bath for 10 minutes.

Banana Jam

Yield: 8 half-pints

6½ pounds very ripe bananas
2¼ cups honey
1 cup orange juice
¾ cup lemon juice

Peel and remove any bruised or decayed sections of the bananas. Slice the bananas about ¼-inch thick to measure 3 quarts. Combine the bananas, honey and juices in a large kettle. Bring to a boil and cook, stirring constantly, for 10 minutes. Reduce heat and simmer, stirring frequently, for about 15 minutes. Remove from heat and spoon hot mixture into hot sterilized jars to within ¼-inch from the top. Complete seals. Process in a boiling-water bath for 15 minutes.

This is an unusual jam which can be made any time of the year.

Bing Cherry Jam

Yield: 3 half-pints

4 cups pitted cherries
1½ cups honey
2 tablespoons lemon juice
¼ teaspoon salt

Pit cherries and combine with honey, lemon juice, and salt in a kettle. Bring to a boil over medium heat, stirring constantly. Boil rapidly over high heat, about 9°F above boiling for 15 minutes. It thickens more as it cools. Spoon hot jam into hot sterilized jars to within ¼-inch from top. Complete seals. Process 10 minutes in a boiling-water bath.

Great as a cheesecake topping!

Blackberry Jam

Yield: 8 half-pints

9 cups berries, mashed
4¼ cups honey
3 sticks agar-agar
2 cups berry juice
1 cup water

(May also use chokecherries, boysenberries, gooseberries, loganberries, or youngberries.)

Soak agar-agar in juice and water for 15 minutes, then cook mixture over low heat for 15 minutes. Add fruit and bring to 9°F above boiling. Add honey; cook for 10 minutes at this temperature. Spoon hot jam into hot sterilized jars to within ¼-inch from top. Seal. Process in a boiling-water bath for 15 minutes.

Blackberry-Huckleberry Jam

Yield: 8 half-pints

5 cups blackberries
4 cups huckleberries
3 sticks agar-agar
2 cups berry juice
1 cup water
4½ cups honey

Soak agar-agar in the juice and water for 15 minutes, then cook mixture over low heat for 15 minutes. Add fruit and bring to 9°F above boiling. Add honey. Cook 10 minutes at this temperature. Spoon hot jam into hot sterilized jars to within ¼-inch from top. Seal. Process in a boiling-water bath for 15 minutes.

This jam has a full-bodied flavor—a good firm jam.

Mountain Mamma's Trail Jam

Yield: 1¼ cups

1 cup berries
⅓ cup honey
1 tablespoon lemon juice

Mash the berries in a pan and heat to a boil. Add the honey and lemon juice. Bring to a good rolling boil and cook at this temperature for 5-10 minutes until it begins to thicken.

Eat and enjoy! This jam can be made over the camp stove, even while on a backpacking trip.

Blueberry-Loganberry Jam

Yield: 7 half-pints

1½ cups blueberries, fresh or frozen
2 cups honey
2 cups loganberry wine
2 tablespoons frozen
  orange juice concentrate
2 sticks agar-agar (½ oz.)

Mash the blueberries. Combine juice from the berries with the wine and orange juice concentrate. Add the agar-agar. Let sit for 15 minutes, then stir and heat to a simmer. Cook for 15 minutes over low heat. Add the honey and blueberries. Bring to a rolling boil, about 9°F/5°C above boiling, and let boil hard for 5 minutes, stirring constantly. Remove from heat, stir and skim for 5 minutes. Spoon hot mixture into hot sterilized jars. Complete seals. Process in a boiling-water bath for 5 minutes.

Blue's Blueberry Jam

Yield: 3 pints

8 cups blueberries, stemmed
2 cups water
4 cups honey 3 C.
2 cups currants

To prepare currants for use in this recipe, cook them slowly in 2 cups water for 10 minutes and press through a sieve to remove seeds. Set aside. Combine berries and water. Cook slowly for 5 minutes. Bring to a **rapid** boil and cook for 5 minutes. Stir in currants. Add honey, stirring occasionally until it dissolves. Cook until thick, about 20 minutes. As mixture thickens, stir often to prevent scorching. Spoon hot jam into hot sterilized jars, to within ½-inch from top. Seal. Process for 15 minutes in a boiling-water bath.

Cranberry-Orange Jam

Yield: 3 pints

1 pound cranberries
3 cups water
¾ cup orange juice
¼ cup lemon juice
2 cups honey

Rinse cranberries well. Put the cranberries and the water in a kettle and bring to a boil. Reduce heat and simmer uncovered for 10 minutes. Drain, but reserve the liquid. Put the berries in a blender and blend until pureed. Add enough of the reserved liquid to make 4 cups. Return to kettle and stir in the orange juice, lemon juice, and honey. Bring to a rolling boil over a high heat, stirring constantly. Heat to 9°F/5°C above boiling and cook for 8 minutes, until thick. Remove from heat and skim off foam. Spoon hot mixture into hot sterilized jars. Complete seals. Process in a boiling-water bath for 10 minutes.

Special Cranberry Jam

Yield: 4 half-pints

2 cups fresh cranberries
2½ cups frozen strawberries (20 oz.)
½ cup water
2 cups honey

Mash cranberries or puree in a blender with the water. Combine with strawberries and cook over low heat for 10 minutes. Add honey. Bring to 9°F/5°C above boiling. Cook rapidly until thick, about 8 minutes. Spoon hot into hot sterilized jars to within ¼-inch from top. Seal. Process for 10 minutes in a boiling-water bath. This is a quick jam to make. These two berries complement each other's flavors very well but frozen strawberries must be used since their seasons do not correspond.

Spicy Cranberry Jam

Yield: 7 half-pints

2 lbs. cranberries (8 cups)
1 cup water
1 cup apple cider vinegar
1½ teaspoons ground cinnamon
½ teaspoon ground cloves
½ teaspoon ground allspice
4½ cups honey

Mash cranberries and combine with water and vinegar. (It helps to puree berries in a blender. This also grinds the skins so the berries need not be pressed through a sieve.) Cook until soft—about 45 minutes. Put through a coarse strainer. Retain the liquid, which is thick, and discard the pulp. Add spices and honey to liquid. Rapidly bring to a boil. Cook 8 minutes, or until thick. Spoon hot into hot sterilized jars to within ¼-inch from top. Seal. Process in a boiling-water bath for 10 minutes.

This jam turns a beautiful, deep velvet, crimson red at the gel point, and is a special treat to make on a rainy winter day. It fills the house with spicy smells and steams the windows with its goodness!

Winter's Delight

Yield: 5 half-pints

3 cups cranberries
1½ cups diced apples (peeled)
1½ cups water
1½ cups crushed pineapple (undrained)
  which equals about one small pineapple
2 tablespoons lemon juice
2⅓ cups honey

Put cranberries in a blender to mash and grind skins, or mash and, after first cooking, press through sieve to remove skins. Cook apples and cranberries in the water until tender, about 45 minutes. Measure out 3 cups of pulp and add pineapple, lemon juice, and honey to it. Mix well and boil rapidly at 9°F above boiling until thick and clear, about 8 minutes. Spoon hot into hot sterilized jars to within ¼-inch from top. Seal. Process for 10 minutes in a boiling-water bath.

Honeydew-Ginger Jam

Yield: 4 half-pints

3 cups honeydew melon, coarsely chopped
1½ cups honey
3 tablespoons lemon juice
1 tablespoon finely chopped ginger root

Place melon, honey, lemon juice, and ginger in a pan. Let stand for about 2 hours until a syrup forms. Bring to a boil and boil for 2 minutes, stirring constantly. Reduce the heat and simmer until thickened, about 45 minutes. Stir frequently. Spoon hot mixture into hot sterilized jars. Complete seals. Process in a boiling-water bath for 10 minutes.

Honey-Fig Jam

Yield: 7 half-pints

8 cups figs
4 cups honey
1 lemon

Peel figs, mash them, and cook slowly. (Figs need not be peeled though peeling them will give a nicer quality). When they reach a slow boil, add honey and finely sliced and chopped lemon, including rind. Cook, stirring constantly, until thick. Spoon into hot sterilized jars to within ¼-inch from top. Seal. Process in a boiling-water bath for 10 minutes.

This jam has a unique flavor—it's delicious! Also makes a good filling for fig bars.

Honey Pineapple Jam

Yield: 3 half-pints

1 qt. finely chopped fresh pineapple
  (about one large pineapple)
2 cups honey
½ lemon, thinly sliced

Combine pineapple (including juice) with the lemon. Slowly heat to a boil, stirring occasionally, then cook rapidly until mixture begins to thicken, about 15 minutes. Add honey and continue to cook for 8 to 10 minutes at 9°F/5°C above boiling. Stir frequently. Skim off foam and spoon hot mixture into hot sterilized jars to within ¼-inch from top. Seal. Process in a boiling-water bath for 10 minutes.

This jam is a good one to make during the winter months because pineapples are less expensive then.

Peach Jam

Yield: 6 half-pints

6 cups peaches, quartered and peeled
2 cups honey
1 teaspoon nutmeg
1 teaspoon cinnamon
1 box powdered pectin
juice of one lemon

To peel the peaches, dunk them into hot water for one minute, then into cold water. Skins slip right off. Pit and quarter them. Mash and add pectin. Bring to a boil. Add honey, lemon juice and spices. Bring to 9°F above boiling, and cook at this temperature for 5 minutes. Spoon hot into hot sterilized jars to within ¼-inch from the top. Seal. Process 10 minutes in a boiling-water bath.

Peach Jam with Agar-Agar

Yield: 8 half-pints

9 cups peaches, quartered and peeled
2½ sticks agar-agar
3 cups honey
juice of one lemon

To peel the peaches, dunk them into hot water for 1 minute, then into cold water. Skins slip right off. Pit and quarter them; measure out 9 cups, then mash. Pour off 2 cups of the juice. Soak the agar-agar in the juice for 15 minutes, then simmer slowly for 15 minutes, stirring often. Place the peaches in a large pan and add the lemon juice and the agar-agar mixture. Bring to a boil and add the honey. Return to a boil and heat to 9°F/5°C above boiling, and cook at this temperature for 10 minutes. Spoon hot into hot sterilized jars to within ¼-inch from the top. Seal. Process for 10 minutes in a boiling-water bath.

Pear-Pineapple Jam

Yield: 8 half-pints

3 pounds ripe pears (9 cups)
1 cup crushed pineapple and its juice
grated rind of one lemon or lime
3¾ cups honey

Wash, pare, core, and seed pears. Cut finely and combine with pineapple. Add lemon or lime rind and honey; cook slowly over medium heat until honey dissolves. Bring to a boil and cook for 8 minutes at 9°F above boiling, stirring frequently. Skim off foam and spoon hot mixture into hot sterilized jars to within ¼-inch from top. Seal. Process in a boiling-water bath for 10 minutes.

Pineapple Jam

Yield: 4 half-pints

1 qt. finely chopped pineapple
1¼ cups honey
1 cup water
½ lemon, thinly sliced

Combine all ingredients. Slowly bring to a boil, stirring occasionally. Cook rapidly until thick, about 30 minutes. Stir frequently as mixture thickens to prevent scorching. Spoon hot mixture into hot sterilized jars to within ¼-inch from top. Complete seal. Process in a boiling-water bath for 10 minutes.

Plum Jam

Yield: 4 half-pints

4 cups plums, pitted
1¾ cups honey

Wash plums and remove pits. Put plums in the blender or chop them finely. Combine with the honey and let sit for 1 hour. Bring to a boil over medium heat and boil rapidly for 10 to 15 minutes. Spoon hot mixture into hot sterilized jars. Complete seal. Process in a boiling-water bath for 10 minutes. Mariposa, Queen Ann, Duarte, and Santa Rosa are excellent varieties to use.

Plum-Date Jam

Yield: 8 half-pints

9 cups plums
2 stick agar-agar
2¼ cups date sugar
2 cups water
½ cup lemon juice
1 cup water

Pit plums, cut and mash. Soak agar-agar for 15 minutes in 1 cup of the juice and 1 cup water. Cook over low heat for 15 minutes. Add to plums; bring rapidly to a boil. Stir in date sugar and lemon juice and boil rapidly for 15 minutes. Spoon hot mixture into hot sterilized jars to within ¼-inch of top. Complete seal. Process in a boiling-water bath for 15 minutes.

Raspberry-Plum Jam

Yield: 6 pints

*2½ lbs. Santa Rosa plums
  (about 4 cups after pitting)
3 cups raspberries, fresh or frozen
5 cups honey
½ cup lemon juice
3 sticks agar-agar
½ cup water*

Mash the berries and combine their juice with the water. Break up the agar-agar and soak for 15 minutes in the juice and water. Simmer this mixture for 15 minutes. Meanwhile, cut the plums in half and remove their pits. Finely chop them and place them in a large kettle. Add the raspberries and begin to cook. Add the agar-agar mixture and bring to a boil over high heat. Stir frequently as the mixture begins to thicken. Add the honey and lemon juice. Bring to 9°F/5°C above boiling and cook for 5 minutes. Remove from heat; skim off foam. Spoon hot mixture into hot sterilized jars to within ¼-inch from top. Complete seals. Process for 10 minutes in a boiling-water bath.

Raspberry Jam

Yield: 3 half-pints

*3 cups raspberries
1½ cups honey*

Mash berries in a sauce pan. Heat to a boil and cook down for 15 minutes. Add the honey and bring to 9°F/5°C above boiling. Cook for 5 minutes. Remove from heat and beat with a wire whip for about 6 minutes. Spoon into hot jars to within ¼-inch from top. Complete seals. Process in a boiling-water bath for 10 minutes.

Rose Hip Jam

Yield: 3 half-pints

1 lb. rose hips
1 cup water
1½ cups honey

Simmer rose hips in the water until fruit is tender. Rub through a sieve. Return to heat and add honey. Simmer until thick, stirring frequently. Spoon hot into hot sterilized jars. Seal. Process in a boiling-water bath for 10 minutes.

Rose hips should be gathered after the first frost of autumn.

Strawberry Jam

Yield: 7 half-pints

6 cups strawberries
2 cups honey
¼ cup lemon juice
1 box powdered pectin

Mash berries and add pectin, stirring well to dissolve. Bring to a boil. Stir in honey and lemon juice. Bring to 9°F/5°C above boiling and cook for 5 minutes. Spoon off scum. Spoon hot mixture into hot sterilized jars to within ¼-inch from top. Seal. Process for 15 minutes in a boiling-water bath. (5 supermarket baskets of berries equals about 6 cups.)

Strawberry Jam with Agar-Agar

Yield: 8 half-pints

3 teaspoons lemon juice
2½ sticks agar-agar (¾ oz.)
9 cups strawberries
3 cups honey
2 cups strawberry juice
1 cup water

Stem berries and cut in half. Extract 2 cups of juice by mashing the berries or pressing through a strainer. Combine the juice with the water and soak the agar-agar in it for 15 minutes. Then simmer it for 15 minutes, stirring often. Add the berries and bring to a boil. Add the honey and lemon juice, stirring well. Bring to 9°F/5°C above boiling. Cook at this temperature for 5 minutes. Skim the foam from the top. Spoon hot into hot sterilized jars to ¼-inch from top. Complete seals. Process in a boiling-water bath for 15 minutes. (8 baskets of berries equals 9 cups of berries.)

This is an excellent jam which holds its shape and is not too sweet.

Tart Apricot-Pineapple Jam

Yield: 10 half-pints

4 cups dried apricots
5 cups pineapple, crushed or
* in small chunks (2 pineapples)*
1 cup pineapple juice (obtained
* from crushing)*
1 lemon, thinly sliced and chopped
* (including rind)*

Simmer apricots in enough water to cover until they are soft enough to be mashed. Add pineapple and lemon. Simmer, stirring frequently, until the mixture is thick and the pineapple chunks are clear. Add juice while simmering. Pour into hot sterilized jars to within ¼-inch from top. Seal and process in a boiling-water bath for 10 minutes.

This is an interesting tart jam that makes a nice variation to the usual sweet jams. It is delicious spread on crisp bread.

Apple Jelly

6 lbs. apples, coarsely chopped
honey

Boil apples in enough water to cover until they are mushy, then strain through a jelly bag. For every pint of juice add 1 pound of honey. Boil to the gel point. Spoon into hot sterilized jars. Complete seals. Let stand at room temperature for 24 hours to set.

Peach Jelly

3¾ lbs. peaches or 3 cups peach juice
2½ cups honey
½ cup water
1 box powdered pectin

Crush the peaches, removing the pits, but do not remove the skins. Add them to the water and simmer for 5 minutes. Drain through a jelly bag. Place 3 cups of the juice in a large kettle, add the pectin and stir vigorously. Place over medium heat and bring to boiling point. Add honey and boil until gel point is reached. Spoon into hot sterilized jars. Complete seals. Let stand at room temperature for 24 hours to set.

Wine Jelly

Yield: 4 half-pints

1¾ cups wine (⅘ pt.)
1½ cups mild honey
1 cup apple pectin (see recipe for pectin
 on page 47) or 3 oz. liquid pectin

Mix the wine and honey and bring to a rolling boil. Add the pectin and again bring to a good boil. Cook at that temperature for 2 minutes, stirring constantly. Remove from the heat and skim with a metal spoon. Pour hot mixture into hot sterilized jars; seal. Let them stand at room temperature until the jelly has set (about 24 hours).

This jelly is a great complement to cheese and crackers. For a deep red jelly try a Ruby Port, Zinfandel, Cabernet Sauvignon, or Vino Rosso. For a rosy jelly try a fruity Rosé wine.

Spicy Port Wine Jelly

Yield: 8 half-pints

2 cups port wine
3 cups honey
⅛ teaspoon cinnamon
⅛ teaspoon cloves
3 oz. liquid pectin or
 1 cup apple pectin (see recipe on p. 47)

Combine wine, honey, cinnamon and cloves and bring to a full rolling boil. Add the pectin and again bring to a good boil. Cook at this temperature for 2 minutes, stirring constantly. Remove pan from heat and skim with a metal spoon. Pour into hot sterilized jars. Seal and let stand at room temperature until jelly has set—about 24 hours.

Honey Jelly

2½ cups honey
½ cup water
½ cup liquid pectin

Combine honey and water. Bring just to boiling point, heating slowly to prevent scorching. Remove from heat, add pectin slowly, stirring constantly. Pour at once into hot sterilized jars. Complete seals and let stand at room temperature for 24 hours.

Apricot Preserves [sun-cooked]

3 lbs. apricots (6 cups)
2 cups honey
¼ cup lemon juice

Proceed as for berries (see page 65).

Berry Preserves

Yield: 4 pints

5 pounds berries (3 heaping quarts)
5 cups honey

Wash berries; cook slowly until the juice is extracted. Add the honey, then boil rapidly for 20 minutes. Pour hot mixture into hot sterilized jars to within ½-inch from top. Seal and process in a boiling-water bath for 10 minutes.

Sun-Cooked Berry Preserves

Yield: 5 ½-pints

6 cups berries
2 cups honey
¼ cup lemon juice

Blackberries, blueberries, boysenberries, currants, mulberries, gooseberries, raspberries, strawberries may be used. This preserve is a sun-cooked jam made by solar energy. You need a **hot** still day. Have a table set up in full sun. As when drying fruit, set the table legs in pans of water to keep crawling insects off. Have a clean piece of glass set at an angle over the area where the jam will set, and use mosquito netting or cheesecloth to protect the other three sides. Place the berries, honey, and lemon juice in a pan. Stir gently, cover and let stand at room temperature for one hour so the juice will start drawing. Place over medium heat and bring to a boil. Cook for 10 minutes. Remove from heat and pour into shallow pans, about ½-inch deep. Place under the glass in full sun. Turn the mixture a few times during the day. If the sun is not hot enough it might take 2 days, so bring the pans in at night. The preserves are ready when the fruit is plump and the syrup is thick. The preserves can be stored in the refrigerator for up to 4 weeks. They can also be canned or frozen. To can them, sterilize 5 half-pint jars and fill with the mixture. Complete seals and process in a boiling-water bath for 10 minutes. To freeze them, pack into freezer containers to within 1 inch of the tops, seal, and freeze.

Cantaloupe Preserves

Yield: 4 half-pints

2 lbs. firm ripe cantaloupe
3 cups light honey
juice of l lemon

Peel cantaloupe and cut into thin slices about 1 inch long. Combine honey and cantaloupe. Let stand overnight. Add lemon juice, cook gently until clear. Spoon hot mixture into hot sterilized jars to within ½-inch from top. Seal and process for 5 minutes in a boiling-water bath.

This is a mid-winter treat over home-made ice cream!

Fig Preserves

Yield: 10 pints

4½ lbs. fresh figs, peeled
  (about 2 quarts)
3¼ cups honey
¼ cup lemon juice
2 lemons, thinly sliced
1½ qts. hot water

The figs should be ripe but still slightly firm. Peeled figs yield a higher quality, but unpeeled figs may also be used. (Unpeeled figs should be covered with water, boiled for 15 to 20 minutes, and drained before adding syrup.) To prepare the syrup, add the honey and lemon juice to the boiling water and cook until the honey has dissolved. Add the figs and cook rapidly for 10 minutes. Stir occasionally. Add the sliced lemons and continue cooking until the figs are clear—about 15 minutes. Pour into a shallow pan and let stand 12 to 24 hours in a cool place. Spoon mixture into sterilized jars. Complete seals and process in a boiling-water bath for 30 minutes. As a variation, sliced ginger root may be added instead of the sliced lemon during the last 15 minutes of cooking.

Ginger-Pear Preserves

Yield: 5 half-pints

4 cups pears, peeled and coarsely chopped
2½ cups honey
¼ teaspoon salt
1 lemon, finely diced
ginger root

Combine all ingredients except ginger root. Cook for about 15 minutes, stirring occasionally, until the mixture is of spreading consistency. Spoon hot into hot sterilized jars to within ½-inch from top. Add a small piece of ginger to each jar. Seal and process in a boiling-water bath for 5 minutes.

Mulberry Preserves

Yield: 4 pints

6 lbs. berries (4 quarts)
3½ cups honey

Wash berries; cook slowly until the juice is extracted, about 20 minutes. Add the honey, then boil rapidly for 20 minutes. Stir often. Pour into sterilized jars to within ½-inch of top. Complete seals and process in a boiling-water bath for 10 minutes.

Peach Preserves

Yield: 7 half-pints

*2 qts. peeled, sliced peaches
  (about 10 large)*
5 cups honey

Combine fruit and honey. Let stand 12 hours in a cool place then bring slowly to a boil, stirring frequently. Boil gently until fruit becomes clear and syrup thickens—about 40 minutes. Stir frequently to prevent sticking. Skim. Spoon hot mixture into hot sterilized jars to within ¼-inch from top. Seal and process for 15 minutes in a boiling-water bath.

A delightful combination with yogurt. For variation add: 3 drops almond extract or 1½ teaspoons ground ginger, nutmeg, or cloves.

Peach or Nectarine Preserves [sun-cooked]

*3 lbs. peeled peaches or nectarines
  (about 6 cups)*
2 cups honey
½ cup lemon juice

Peel the fruit and proceed as for berries. (*see page* 65).

Pineapple Preserves

Yield: 4 half-pints

2 lbs. pineapple (6 cups)
2½ cups honey
1 cup water

Cut pineapple into small cubes. Combine it with water and honey in a preserving kettle and cook for 20 minutes. Spoon into sterilized jars to within ½-inch from top. Seal and process in a boiling-water bath for 10 minutes.

Pineapple-Pear Preserves

Yield: 4 cups

6 medium-size Bartlett pears
1 quart crushed pineapple
1½ cups honey

Pare, halve, core and chop pears to get 4 cups of fruit. Combine juice from pineapple with the honey and bring to a boil. Stir to make sure honey is dissolved. Add pears and pineapple. Simmer slowly, uncovered, until thick—about 1 hour. Stir occasionally. Spoon hot into hot sterilized jars. Seal and process in a boiling-water bath for 10 minutes.

Pumpkin Preserves

4 lbs. pumpkin
2 lemons
honey and salt

Peel pumpkin and remove seeds. Cut into ½-inch cubes. Slice lemons, removing seeds but not rind. Put pumpkin and lemon in kettle; add ½ cup honey for every cup of pumpkin. Add a pinch of salt. Stir the mixture well and let it stand overnight. In the morning, boil slowly until pumpkin is tender. Spoon hot mixture into hot sterilized jars to within ½-inch from top. Seal and process in a boiling-water bath for 5 minutes.

Excellent for pies or pumpkin bread.

Raspberry-Currant Preserves

Yield: 4 pints

1½ qts. raspberries
1½ qts. currants
3 cups honey

Wash the berries and cook them until the juice is extracted. Add the honey and boil rapidly for 20 minutes. Spoon into hot sterilized jars to within ½-inch from top. Complete seals and process in a boiling-water bath for 10 minutes.

Strawberry Preserves

Yield: 4 half-pints

1 qt. stemmed strawberries
3 cups light honey
½ cup lemon juice

Combine berries and honey. Let stand 3-4 hours. Bring slowly to a boil, stirring occasionally until honey fully dissolves. Cook rapidly until thick, about 20 minutes. Add lemon juice and cook 10 minutes longer. Spoon hot into hot sterilized jars. Seal and process in a boiling-water bath for 15 minutes.

Heavenly Strawberry Preserves

Yield: 4-5 half-pints

1½ qts. strawberries (stemmed)
2½ cups honey
⅓ cup lemon juice

Mix strawberries and honey. Let sit for 4 hours. Bring slowly to a boil; add lemon juice. Boil rapidly until berries are clear and syrup begins to thicken--about 10 minutes. (Skim as necessary while boiling.) Pour into a shallow pan. Let stand uncovered for 12 hours. Shake pan occasionally so the berries will absorb the syrup and remain plump and whole. Slowly bring fruit mixture back to 9°F above boiling. Spoon into hot sterilized jars to within ¼-inch of top. Complete seals and process for 20 minutes in a hot-water bath.

Summer's Delight Preserves

Yield: 5 half-pints

1 cup stemmed currants
1 cup water
3¾ cups honey
2 cups stemmed loganberries
2 cups stemmed raspberries
2 cups pitted sweet cherries

Crush currants; combine with water and cook until soft. Drain through a jelly bag into a bowl. (Be sure to wet jelly bag first with hot water so it will not absorb the currant juice.) Add honey to currant juice and bring slowly to boiling, stirring until honey is dissolved and cook rapidly for 5 minutes. Add berries and cherries. Cook for 30 minutes, until thick. Spoon hot mixture into hot sterilized jars. Seal and process in a boiling-water bath for 10 minutes.

Tomato Preserves

Yield: 6 half-pints

1½ qts. tomatoes, peeled (about 2 lbs.)
¾ cup water
2 lemons, thinly sliced
3 cups honey
1 piece ginger root
1 tablespoon mixed pickling spices

Put water in kettle. Tie spices in cheese-cloth bag; add to water along with honey and lemon. Simmer 15 minutes; add toma-toes and cook gently until they become clear. Stir occasionally. Remove spice bag. Cover the tomato mixture and let stand 12–18 hours in a cool place. Heat to boil-ing and pack tomatoes and lemon into hot sterilized jars, leaving room for syrup. Boil syrup 2–3 minutes or longer if too thin. Pour boiling hot over tomatoes, leav-ing ¼-inch headspace. Seal and process 10 minutes in boiling-water bath.

Makes a delicious, unusual spread on toast!

Watermelon Rind Preserves

Yield: 6 half-pints

1½ qts. prepared watermelon rind
4 tablespoons salt
9 cups cold water
1 lemon, sliced thinly
1 tablespoon ground ginger
2 cups honey
¼ cup lemon juice
7 cups water

Prepare watermelon rind by trimming off the green skin and the pink flesh: you want the white part of the rind. Cut it into 1-inch pieces. Dissolve the salt in the 9 cups of water, then add watermelon rind. Let stand for 6 hours. Drain and rinse two times. Cover with cold water and let stand for 30 minutes Drain well. Sprinkle the ginger over the rind, cover with water, and cook until fork-tender. Drain liquid and reserve the rind. Combine the honey and lemon juice in a large pan; add the 7 cups of water. Boil for 5 minutes; add the rind and boil gently for 30 minutes. Add sliced lemon and cook until the melon rind is clear. Spoon hot into hot sterilized jars. Complete seals and process for 20 minutes in a hot-water bath.

Spiced Apple Butter

Yield: 7 half-pints

4 lbs. tart green apples
3 lemons, sliced
2 cups water
2 tablespoons mixed pickling spices
2¾ cups honey
¼ teaspoon salt

Peel, core, and dice apples to make about 3 qts. Place in a kettle along with the sliced lemons and water. Tie pickling spices in a cheesecloth bag and add to apple mixture. Bring to boiling, reduce heat, cover, and simmer about 30 minutes, until apples are tender. Remove spice bag. Push apple mixture through a food mill or sieve to make about 7 cups. Return to kettle, bring to a rapid boil. Add honey and salt; return to the boiling point. Reduce heat slightly and cook uncovered until apple butter thickens—about 20 minutes. Stir frequently. Test as for gel point. Spoon hot into hot sterilized jars. Seal and process in a boiling-water bath for 15 minutes.

Apricot Butter

Yield: 6 half-pints

1½ qts. apricot pulp (about 2 doz. apricots)
2½ cups honey
2 tablespoons lemon juice

To prepare the pulp, cook pitted apricot halves until soft in a small amount of water. Press through a sieve or food mill. Add honey and cook until thick, about 30 minutes. Stir frequently to prevent sticking. Add lemon juice. Spoon hot into hot sterilized jars to within ¼-inch from top. Seal and process for 10 minutes in a boiling-water bath.

Peach Butter

Yield: 4 half-pints

2 cups dried peaches
¾ cup honey
2 cups water

Soak peaches in the water for several hours. Cook in same water very slowly until soft enough to mash into a pulp. Mash and add the honey. Simmer slowly, stirring frequently, until thick. Spoon hot into hot sterilized jars to within ½-inch from top. Seal and process in a boiling-water bath for 10 minutes. You may add ½ teaspoon nutmeg and ½ teaspoon cinnamon along with the honey for a variation.

Plum Butter

Yield: 8 half-pints

5 lbs. ripe plums
½ cup water
3 cups honey

Choose fully ripe but not over-ripe plums. Wash the plums and remove the stems, but leave them whole. Cook over low heat with the ½ cup of water until the plums burst. The juice will flow freely and the pulp will separate from the pits. Shake kettle frequently to prevent sticking. Rub fruit through a puree sieve to remove pits and skin. If the pulp is thin, cook it until it will mound up on a spoon. You should have 8-10 cups of pulp. Add the honey to the pulp. Mix well; heat to boiling and boil vigorously, stirring constantly until it will not separate any juice when placed on a cold saucer. Boiling time should be about 30 minutes. Spoon hot mixture into hot sterilized jars. Complete seals and process in a boiling-water bath for 10 minutes.

For a variation, add ½ teaspoon ground cinnamon for each 4 cups of pulp when the honey is added.

Spiced Nectarine Butter

Yield: About 5 half-pints

4 lbs. nectarines
½ cup water
1¾ cups honey
1 teaspoon cinnamon
½ teaspoon cloves
¼ teaspoon salt

Cut nectarines to make about 2 quarts fruit. Place in kettle along with the water. Bring to boiling point; reduce heat. Cover and simmer until nectarines are tender—about 20 minutes. Push through a food mill or sieve to make about 5 cups of pureed nectarines. Return to kettle and bring to a rapid boil. Add honey; return to boiling point. Reduce heat slightly and cook uncovered until nectarine butter thickens—about 20 minutes. Stir frequently; add cinnamon, cloves and salt. Spoon hot into hot sterilized jars. Seal and process in a boiling-water bath for 15 minutes. Peaches or plums may also be prepared in this manner.

Apple-Cranberry-Pineapple Conserve

Yield: 9 half-pints

5 large apples
3 cups cranberries
2½ cups crushed pineapple
1 orange
1 lemon
2¾ cups honey
1 package powdered pectin
¼ cup slivered almonds

Wash cranberries. Core and cut the unpeeled apples into quarters. Put the cranberries and apples in a blender and blend until finely chopped. Grate the peels of the orange and lemon and juice them. Finely chop or crush the pineapple. Put all of these ingredients into a kettle and bring to a boil. Add the pectin and return to a boil. Add the honey, stirring constantly. Bring to a rolling boil, and boil for one minute. Remove from heat, stir, and skim for 5 minutes. Stir in the almonds. Spoon into hot sterilized jars to within ½-inch from top. Complete seals and process for 5 minutes in a boiling-water bath.

Blueberry-Apple Conserve

Yield: 6 half-pints

1 qt. stemmed blueberries
4 medium-size tart apples
  (about 1 qt. chopped)
½ cup raisins
3 cups honey
¼ cup lemon juice
¼ cup chopped nuts

Core and chop the apples. Combine all ingredients except the nuts. Cook rapidly for about 20 minutes or until thick. Stir frequently as mixture thickens. Add the nuts during the last 5 minutes of cooking. Spoon into hot sterilized jars to within ½-inch from top. Complete seals and process in a boiling-water bath for 10 minutes.

Cantaloupe-Peach Conserve

Yield: 6 half-pints

4 cups peaches
4 cups cantaloupe
4 lemons
3 cups honey
1 cup walnuts

Peel and dice cantaloupe and peaches. Juice the lemons and grate their rinds. Put cantaloupe, peaches, and lemon juice and rind in a kettle. Bring to a boil. Add the honey and cook until thick and clear. Add nuts during last 5 minutes of cooking. Spoon into hot sterilized jars to within ½-inch from top. Complete seals and process in a boiling-water bath for 5 minutes.

Dried Fruit Conserve

Yield: 5 half-pints

1½ cups dried apricots (½ lb.)
1½ cups dried peaches (½ lb.)
1½ cups dried pears (½ lb.)
1 medium orange
3 cups water
1 cup honey
½ cup raisins
1 tablespoon lemon juice
½ teaspoon ground cinnamon
⅛ teaspoon ground cloves
½ cup chopped walnuts

Chop the orange including the peel and cut the dried fruits. Combine in a large kettle with the water. Cover and cook for about 15-20 minutes or until tender. Uncover and add all remaining ingredients, except the nuts. Slowly heat to a boil, stirring occasionally. Cook rapidly until thick—about 15 minutes. Add the nuts during the last 5 minutes of cooking. Spoon into hot sterilized jars. Complete seals and process in a boiling-water bath for 10 minutes.

Gooseberry-Rhubarb Conserve

Yield: 4 half-pints

1½ lbs. gooseberries
1 lb. rhubarb
2 cups honey
¾ cup chopped nuts

Wash gooseberries and stem them. Cut rhubarb into small pieces. Combine the fruits in a kettle. Add the honey and bring to a boil. Cook rapidly until thick, about 20 minutes. Add the nuts for the last five minutes of cooking. Spoon hot mixture into hot sterilized jars to within ½-inch from top. Complete seals and process in a boiling-water bath for 10 minutes.

Orange-Pineapple Conserve

Yield: 4 half-pints

4 oranges
4 cups crushed pineapple
2 cups honey
3 tablespoons chopped nuts

Wash and peel the oranges. Cut the peels into thin slices and measure out 2 cups. Cover the peels with water and boil for 5 minutes. Drain water and repeat this process twice. Cut orange flesh into small pieces, removing the seeds and the rag portion. Add the honey to the orange peels and bring to a boil. Add orange and pineapple; bring to a rolling boil and boil rapidly for 30 minutes. Add nuts during the last 5 minutes of cooking. Spoon into hot sterilized jars to within ½-inch from top. Complete seals and process in a boiling-water bath for 10 minutes

Peach-Prune Conserve

Yield: 4 half-pints

4 cups chopped peaches
½ cup chopped pitted prunes, uncooked
⅓ cup raisins
1 medium orange, seeded and juiced,
  and the peel grated
½ cup water
1 cup honey
¼ cup chopped nuts

Put the peaches, prunes, raisins, orange, and water in a saucepan. Bring to a boil, reduce heat, and cook for about an hour, until thick and dark. Add the honey and cook a few minutes longer until it has dissolved. Add the nuts and cook 5 minutes longer. Spoon hot mixture into hot sterilized jars to within ½-inch from top. Complete seals and process in a boiling-water bath for 10 minutes.

Pear Conserve

Yield: 6 pints

5 lbs. firm pears (15 cups)
5 cups honey
2 cups raisins
½ cup orange rind, cut fine
1 cup orange juice
4 tablespoons lemon juice
½ cup chopped nuts

Peel pears and cut into small pieces. Add the honey and let stand overnight. Next morning, add the raisins, orange rind and juice, and lemon juice. Bring to a boil and cook until thick—about 30 minutes. Add the nuts during the last 5 minutes of cooking. Spoon hot mixture into hot sterilized jars to within ½-inch from top. Complete seals and process in a boiling-water bath for 10 minutes.

Raspberry-Cherry Conserve

Yield: 4 half-pints

2 cups raspberries
6 cups cherries, pitted
1¼ cups honey
¼ cup chopped walnuts

Put raspberries and cherries in a kettle and cook until the mixture begins to thicken. Add the honey and cook for about 15 minutes. Add the walnuts and cook for 5 minutes more. Spoon into hot sterilized jars to within ½-inch from top. Complete seals and process in a boiling-water bath for 5 minutes.

Strawberry-Rhubarb Conserve

Yield: 7 half-pints

4 cups rhubarb
4 cups strawberries
1/3 cup chopped walnuts
3½ cups honey

Wash and cut about 2½ lbs. rhubarb into ½-inch pieces. Wash and stem 1 qt. strawberries. Measure 4 cups of each into the kettle. Add honey and heat slowly to a boil, stirring occasionally. Cook rapidly until thick—about 20-25 minutes. Stir occasionally while cooking. Stir in nuts during last 5 minutes of cooking. Remove from heat and stir for a few minutes; skim off foam. Spoon hot into hot sterilized jars to within ½-inch from tops. Seal. Process in a boiling-water bath for 10 minutes.

Tomato Conserve

Yield: 4 pints

18 cups ripe tomatoes (about 6 lbs.)
4 teaspoons ground ginger
3 cups honey
3 lemons, thinly sliced

Cook the tomatoes for about 45 minutes. Add the honey, ginger, and lemons. Cook until thick and smooth. Spoon hot mixture into hot sterilized jars to within ½-inch from top. Complete seals and process in a boiling-water bath for 10 minutes.

Amber Marmalade

Yield: 10 half-pints

3 cups thinly sliced grapefruit peel
  (about 2 grapefruits)
1 cup thinly sliced orange peel
  (about 2 oranges)
3 cups grapefruit pulp, chopped
1½ cups orange pulp, chopped
1 cup thinly sliced lemon
  (about 2 medium lemons)
water
6½ cups honey

Cook the fruit peel in enough water to cover. Boil for 5 minutes, then drain and repeat. Add the fruit pulp and lemon to the drained peel and about 3 qts. of water. Bring to a boil and cook for 5 minutes. Remove from heat, cover and let stand for 16 hours in a cool place. Then bring to a boil and cook rapidly for 35 minutes. Add the honey and slowly bring mixture to a boil. Boil rapidly for about 30 minutes until the mixture reaches the gel point. Spoon hot into hot sterilized jars to within ½-inch from tops. Complete seals and process in a boiling-water bath for 10 minutes.

Carrot-Orange Marmalade

Yield: 10 half-pints

2 medium-size oranges
4 cups grated carrots
4 lemons
6 cups water
5 cups honey

Juice the oranges and the lemons. Reserve the juice. Grate the rind of 1 orange and 2 lemons. Put the grated rinds and the grated carrots into a kettle along with the water. Cook until tender—about 15 minutes. Add the juices to this mixture. Bring to a boil and cook down for about 30 minutes. Stir in the honey and continue to cook at a rapid boil for 15-20 minutes, until thick. Spoon hot mixture into hot sterilized jars to within ½-inch from top. Complete seals and process in a boiling-water bath for 10 minutes.

Grapefruit Marmalade

Yield: 6 half-pints

1⅓ cups thinly sliced grapefruit peel
2⅔ cups chopped grapefruit pulp
8 cups water
2 cups honey

Cover the sliced grapefruit peel with water. Boil for 10 minutes; drain and repeat 3 times. After the final cooking, add the chopped pulp and 8 cups of water to the drained peel. Cover and let stand 16 hours in a cool place. Bring to a boil and cook rapidly for 35–40 minutes until the peel is tender. Add the honey and slowly bring to a boil. Stir occasionally while the honey dissolves. Cook rapidly for about 30 minutes until the mixture reaches the gel point, stirring occasionally to prevent scorching. Spoon hot mixture into hot sterilized jars to within ½-inch from top. Complete seals and process for 10 minutes in a boiling-water bath.

Kumquat Marmalade

Yield: 8 half-pints

3 qts. water
2 dozen kumquats
2 medium oranges
⅓ cup lemon juice
4½ cups honey

Thinly slice the kumquats to measure two cups. Slice the orange peel and the orange pulp to measure 1½ cups each. Add the water to the fruit, cover, and let stand overnight. Bring to a boil and cook until the peel is tender. Add the honey and stir occasionally until it dissolves. Resume a rapid boil and cook about 45 minutes until the mixture reaches the gel point. Stir occasionally to prevent scorching. Spoon into hot sterilized jars to within ½-inch from top. Complete seals and process for 10 minutes in a boiling-water bath.

Orange Marmalade with Pectin

Yield: 6 half-pints

4 medium oranges
1 medium lemon
¼ teaspoon baking soda
3 cups honey
3 oz. liquid pectin

Remove fruit peels and scrape off excess white pulp. Cut the peels into very thin strips and combine them with 1½ cups of water and the soda. Bring this mixture to a boil; reduce heat, cover and cook slowly for 10 minutes. Drain. Remove the white membrane from the fruit. Section the fruit (work over a bowl to catch the juice) and combine fruit and resulting juice in a large pan. Cover and cook slowly for 20 minutes. Remove from heat and measure out 3 cups. In a large pan, combine the 3 cups fruit with the honey. Bring to a boil and cook for 5 minutes, stirring often. Remove from heat and add the liquid pectin. Stir for 5 minutes. Skim mixture, then spoon into hot sterilized jars to within ½-inch from the top. Complete seals and process for 10 minutes in a boiling-water bath.

Orange Marmalade

Yield: 7 half-pints

6 large oranges
2 lemons
3 cups honey
4 cups water

Peel the oranges and thinly slice the peel. Chop the pulp. You should have about 4 cups of each. Thinly slice the lemons to measure 1 cup. Combine the fruits with the water and simmer for 5 minutes. Remove from heat, cover, and let stand for 16 hours in a cool place. Then cook rapidly for about 1 hour, until the peel is tender. Add the honey and slowly bring to a boil, stirring occasionally. Cook rapidly for about 25 minutes, until mixture reaches the gel point. As mixture thickens, stir often to prevent scorching. Spoon into hot sterilized jars to within ½-inch from top. Complete seals and process in a boiling-water bath for 10 minutes.

Peach-Orange Marmalade

Yield: 8 half-pints

2 medium oranges
10 large peaches
½ cup lemon juice
2½ cups honey

Slice the orange peel to measure ¾ cup. Chop the orange pulp to measure 1½ cups. Remove the skins from the peaches by blanching them, then chop the peaches to measure about 8 cups. Combine all ingredients except the honey. Slowly bring to a boil and cook for 10 minutes. Stir in the honey and cook rapidly until thick—about 15 minutes. Stir frequently to prevent scorching. Spoon into hot sterilized jars to within ½-inch from top. Complete seals and process in a boiling-water bath for 10 minutes.

Pineapple-Orange Marmalade

Yield: 9 half-pints

1 large pineapple, chopped fine
  (about 6 cups)
6 oranges
1 lemon
3½ cups honey

Thinly slice the oranges and lemon. Add enough water to cover the fruit. Cook gently for 1 hour in a covered pan. Remove from heat and let stand for 16 hours in a cool place. Add the pineapple to the mixture and cook until tender. Add the honey and slowly bring to a boil, stirring occasionally. Cook rapidly until thick. Spoon into hot sterilized jars to within ½-inch from top. Complete seals and process for 10 minutes in a boiling-water bath.

Pineapple-Strawberry Marmalade

Yield: 6 half-pints

1 medium pineapple (2½ cups)
4 medium oranges
6 cups strawberries
3½ cups honey
1 teaspoon grated orange peel

Finely chop the pineapple. Chop about 2½ cups of orange pulp and grate part of the peel to measure 1 teaspoon. Combine these ingredients with the honey and slowly bring to a boil. Cook rapidly for 15 minutes, stirring occasionally. Stir in the strawberries and continue cooking rapidly for 25-30 minutes, until the mixture reaches the gel point. Spoon into hot sterilized jars to within ½-inch from the top. Complete seals and process for 10 minutes in a boiling-water bath.

Tomato Marmalade

Yield: 6 half-pints

12 cups tomatoes, cut up
2 oranges
2 lemons
5 cups honey
6 inches of cinnamon stick, broken up
2 tablespoons whole cloves

Remove the skins from the tomatoes by blanching. Cut into small pieces. Slice the lemons and oranges very thin, then cut the slices into pieces. Put the tomatoes in a large pan, pouring off the juice and reserving for another use. Add the lemons and oranges. Slowly bring to a boil and cook for 5 minutes. Stir in the honey and add the spices, tied loosely in a cheesecloth bag. Boil rapidly for about 45 minutes until the mixture is thick and clear. Remove the spice bag. Spoon into hot sterilized jars to within ½-inch from top. Complete seals and process for 10 minutes in a boiling-water bath.

88 NOTES

Chapter 3

Canned Fruits

Canned Fruits

Fruits, with their delicious flavors, rich colors, and high nutritional value, offer a greater variety of uses than any other product we might can or preserve. They add a pleasing variety to the winter diet.

These fruits may also be used in desserts such as pies, puddings, yogurt, sundaes, and gelatins. Delicious fruit salads can be made from these products to brighten up a dinner or luncheon.

Selection of Fruits

Select fresh, firm, just-ripe fruits for canning. If the produce is even a shade overripe it will float to the top of the jar. Use the fruit as soon as possible after picking to ensure a high-quality product. If you have to hold the fruit over for a day or two, be sure to refrigerate it to stop further ripening.

Syrups for Canning Fruits

Fruits may be packed in a honey syrup, their own natural juice, or water. Fruits in an unsweetened liquid should be processed just like sweetened fruits. The sweetening helps the produce to hold its flavor, shape and color, but it is not necessary to prevent spoilage. The proportions for a honey syrup are as follows:

Syrup	Honey	Water	Yield
Thin	1½ cups	4 cups	5 cups
Medium	2 cups	4 cups	5½ cups
Heavy	3 cups	4 cups	6 cups

To Prevent Darkening of Fruits

Changes in the color, flavor, and Vitamin C content of fruit during canning are caused by oxidation. No browning will occur in fruit tissues until practically all of the ascorbic acid (Vitamin C) has been oxidized.

Vitamin C, either as rose hip concentrate or ascorbic acid, added to light-colored fruits is a good anti-oxidant. Put 250 milligrams of Vitamin C in the bottom of each quart jar before packing fruit or add ½ teaspoon of crystalline ascorbic acid to each quart of syrup before pouring it over the fruit in the jars.

To prevent darkening while you are preparing the fruit for packing, the following process may be used. As soon as the fruit is washed and sliced, drop it into a solution of 2 tablespoons lemon juice or vinegar and 2 tablespoons salt to a gallon of water. Allow to soak for no longer than 20 minutes, then rinse well in cold water before packing.

Blanching Fruit and Cold Dip

Blanching means plunging produce such as peaches, apricots, tomatoes, beets or carrots into boiling water for a short time. It is best to use a stainless steel wire basket to hold the fruit. Lower it into boiling water for one minute, then immediately into cold water for 5 to 10 seconds. The cold dip will make handling easier, as the produce is very hot after blanching. This whole process actually shrinks the fruit and loosens the skins for easy peeling. Fruits quickly lose valuable nutrients after they are peeled. Blanching to remove the skins seals in most of the nutrients and the color.

Methods of Packing Fruits

Fruits may be packed either by the hot pack or the raw pack method described in Chapter One. More food can be packed into the jars when the hot pack method is used because the food has already shrunk slightly due to moisture loss; however, the additional heating also causes foods to lose some of their nutritional value. Foods which are raw packed hold their shapes better and pack more easily. This is desirable when packing peaches, apricots, pears, or apples, which must be overlapped in the jars to avoid air pockets. Both methods require processing in a boiling-water bath. Processing times are listed with each recipe.

Fruit Preparation for the Boiling-water Bath

Fill the canning kettle over half full with warm water, deep enough to cover the containers. Begin to heat to boiling. Wash the jars and place them in the canning kettle to sterilize. Leave them there until needed. Pour boiling water over the rings and seals. Set aside until needed.

Prepare syrup, if it is to be used. If packing in water or juice, prepare the liquid and have it hot. Prepare the fruit for canning as described in the recipe.

Pack the fruit, either raw or hot, into the sterilized jars. Remove the sterilized jars from the canning kettle one by one, replacing them as soon as they are packed and sealed. Pack the fruit to within 1 inch from the top and cover with hot syrup or hot water to within ½-inch from the top. To remove any air bubbles from the jars, run a sterilized spatula or knife along the side of the jar, pressing the fruit gently as you do so. Do not move the knife through the middle of the contents as it could create air pockets. Wipe the sealing edge clean with a hot sponge or towel. Complete the seal by immediately placing a lid on the jar and screwing it down firmly with a band. Repeat this process until you have filled all the jars in the kettle.

Lower the rack gently into the kettle. The water should be 1 to 2 inches above the tops of the containers. If necessary, add boiling water, being careful not to pour the water directly onto the containers. Put the lid on the kettle; begin to count the processing time as soon as the water starts to boil. Process as recommended in each recipe. For higher altitudes, increase the processing time one minute for each 1,000 feet above sea level (see table on page 46). Boil gently and steadily; add more boiling water if necessary to keep the containers covered.

As soon as the processing time is up, remove the jars from the canning kettle. Place them on a wire rack or a folded towel a few inches from one another to allow for good air circulation and allow to cool for 12 hours. Do not put them in a draft. Test the seal by pressing the lid with your finger. If it stays down when pressed, the jar is sealed correctly. If it pops back, the jar is not sealed. If a jar has failed to seal, repack and reprocess it using a new lid. The product may also be refrigerated for use within a few days. Store sealed jars in a cool, dry, dark place.

Helpful Hints

1. Always have fruit and syrup ready, the canning kettle filled with hot water, and the jars sterilized before you begin packing any jars.

2. Lye is a highly caustic alkaline compound which is also known as caustic soda. Although almost all commercial canneries use lye for removal of skins, you should avoid it since it is a quick destroyer of Vitamin C and many of the B-complex vitamins.

3. To remove skins from fruits or berries, use the blanching method, followed by a cold dip. The skins will slip right off.

4. Keep the water hot in the canning kettle if you are planning to do a second batch on the same day.

5. Fruit at the top of a jar with too much headroom or too little liquid will tend to darken.

6. Traditionally it has been said that tomatoes' natural-acid content makes them "safe" to categorize as a high-acid food. This is no longer completely true. Some varieties of hybrid tomatoes may not be high enough in acid to be safe. Try to use non-hybrids or test the acid content (pH level).

7. Tomato seeds have a tendency to creep up around the sealing edge. To prevent this from occuring, be sure to wipe the sealing edge and inside rim of the jar clean.

Yield of Canned Fruit from Fresh

Fruit	Amount Required for 1 Quart Canned Fruit	Measure Per Pound
Apples	2½-3 pounds	3 cups, sliced
Apricots	2-2½ pounds	2 cups, halved
Berries		
Blackberries	5-8 cups	1½ cups
Boysenberries	5-8 cups	1½ cups
Huckleberries	5-8 cups	3⅔ cups
Loganberries	5-8 cups	3½ cups
Raspberries	5-8 cups	3¼ cups
Strawberries	6-8 cups	2⅔ cups
Youngberries	5-8 cups	2⅔ cups
Cherries		
Unpitted	6-8 cups	3 cups, stemmed
Pitted	5-6 cups	2½ cups, stemmed
Cranberries	5-8 cups	4 cups
Currants	5-8 cups	1¼ cups
Figs—peeled & chopped	5-8 cups	1¾ cups
Gooseberries	6-8 cups	2⅔ cups
Grapes	6-8 cups	2½ cups, stemmed
Peaches	2-2½ pounds	1½ cups, sliced
Pears	2-2½ pounds	1¾ cups, sliced
Plums	2-2½ pounds	2 cups, halved
Prunes, fresh	2-2½ pounds	2 cups, halved
Rhubarb, cut	5-8 cups	3 cups, sliced
Tomatoes	2½-3 pounds	3 cups, sliced

Jar Estimation

Fruits	Measure and Weight	Quart Jars Needed	Amount for 1 Quart Jar
Apples	1 bu. (48 lbs.)	16-20	2½ to 3 lbs.
Applesauce	1 bu. (48 lbs.)	15-18	2½ to 3½ lbs.
Apricots	1 lug (22 lbs.)	7-11	2 to 2½ lbs.
Berries	24-quart crate	18-28	1½ to 3 lbs.
Cherries	1 bu. (56 lbs.)	22-32 (unpitted)	2 to 2½ lbs.
	1 lug (22 lbs.)	9-11 (unpitted)	2 to 2½ lbs.
Peaches	1 bu. (48 lbs.)	18-24	2 to 3 lbs.
	1 lug (22 lbs.)	8-12	2 to 3 lbs.
Pears	1 bu. (50 lbs.)	20-25	2 to 3 lbs.
	1 lug (35 lbs.)	14-17	2 to 3 lbs.
Plums	1 bu. (56 lbs.)	24-30	1½ to 2½ lbs.
	1 lug (24 lbs.)	12	1½ to 2½ lbs.

Apples

Yield: 5 quarts

15 lbs. apples
1½ qts. water
1¾ cups honey

Wash, core, peel, and slice the apples. Treat to prevent darkening (see following applesauce recipe) Drain and rinse. Prepare syrup by adding honey to the water and heating until honey is dissolved. Add the apples to the syrup and simmer for 5 minutes. Place hot into hot sterilized jars, leaving a ½-inch headspace. Cover with boiling syrup to within ½-inch from top of jar. Complete seals. Process for 20 minutes in a boiling-water bath. Cinnamon (3 sticks) may be added to the syrup while apples are cooking. Remove them from the syrup before packing into jars.

Spiced Applesauce

Yield: 8 pints

40 large apples
8 cups water
10 inches of cinnamon sticks
1 teaspoon nutmeg
1 teaspoon allspice
juice of 3 lemons

Wash apples. Quarter, core, and peel them. To prevent peeled fruit from darkening while standing several minutes before cooking, drop into a solution of 1 qt. water and 1½ teaspoons salt, then drain. Cook apples in fresh water until soft. Mash. Add cinnamon sticks, nutmeg, allspice and lemon juice. Bring to a boil and remove cinnamon sticks. Spoon hot into hot sterilized jars to ½-inch from top. Complete seals. Process for 25 minutes in a boiling-water bath.

Apricots

Yield: 5 quarts

10 lbs. apricots
1½ qts. water
1¾ cups honey

Wash and halve the apricots. Prepare the syrup by adding honey to water and heating. Pack the fruit into sterilized jars, cavity side down. Fill with the boiling hot syrup to within ½-inch from top. Complete seals. Process pints 20 minutes and quarts 25 minutes in a boiling-water bath.

Berries

Yield: 8 pints

4 lbs. berries
2¼ cups honey

For varieties such as blackberries, blueberries, dewberries, huckleberries, loganberries, mulberries, raspberries and strawberries.

Use only firm-ripe fruit. Wash the berries and combine them with the honey. Let stand for 2 hours. Heat to a boil and cook gently for 5 minutes. Pack into hot sterilized jars. If necessary, add a bit of boiling water to cover the berries. Leave ½-inch of headspace. Process 10 minutes in a boiling-water bath.

Berries contain proportionately more water than larger fruits. For this reason, if the berries are cold-packed they will rise to the top of the jar, while the syrup, being heavier, remains at the bottom. To prevent this, pre-cook the berries as described in this recipe.

Blueberries

Yield: 4 pints

2 lbs. berries

To can these berries for use in pancakes or muffins, put the berries in a square of cheesecloth. Gather together the corners and dip into boiling water. Remove when berry juice begins to appear on the cloth and dip into cold water. Pack into hot jars leaving a ½-inch headspace. It is not necessary to add water, but you may cover with boiling water if desired. Complete seals. Process for 15 minutes in a boiling-water bath.

Spiced Bing Cherries

Yield: 9 pints

8 lbs. cherries, before pitting
6 cups water
2¼ cups honey
½ oz. allspice
4 inches of stick cinnamon

Wash and pit the cherries. If a cherry pitter is not available, you can use a sterilized hairpin or paper clip. Heat the honey with the water and add the spices, tied in a square of cheesecloth. Pour a bit of syrup into each jar. Pack cherries to within ½-inch from top. Fill with boiling syrup to just cover fruit. Complete seals. Process pints for 20 minutes and quarts for 25 minutes in a boiling-water bath.

The cherries are also delicious without the spices.

Royal Anne Cherries

Yield: 3 quarts

5½ lbs. cherries, before pitting
1½ cups honey
4 cups water

Wash and pit cherries. Prepare the syrup by combining honey with water and heating until honey dissolves. Pour a bit of syrup into each jar. Pack the cherries to within ½-inch from top. Fill with boiling syrup to just cover fruit. Complete seals. Process for 25 minutes in a boiling-water bath.

Cranberries

Yield: 6 pints

8 cups cranberries
2 cups honey
4 cups water
2 inches of stick cinnamon
cloves

Wash, sort and stem the berries. Mix together the honey and water. Add the whole spices, tied in a square of cheesecloth, and boil for 3 minutes. Add the cranberries and boil without stirring until the skins burst. Remove the spices. Pour into hot sterilized jars to within ¼-inch from top. Complete seals. Process for 10 minutes in a boiling-water bath.

Cranberry Sauce

Yield: 2 pints

1 qt. cranberries
1 cup water
1 cup honey

Wash the berries. Combine the berries and water and cook until berries are soft. Press through a fine sieve to remove the skins. Add the honey to the berry pulp and bring to a boil. Cook for 3-4 minutes. Spoon into hot sterilized jars to within ½-inch from top. Complete seals. Process for 10 minutes in a boiling-water bath.

Fruit Cocktail

Use any combination of fruits, except for bananas and oranges. Cut fruits into desired sizes. Prepare a light or medium syrup (see p. 93). Pack the fruit into jars and fill to within 1½-inches from the top with the boiling syrup. Complete seals. Process for 15 minutes in a boiling-water bath. Chopped nuts may also be added.

Nectarines

Follow recipe for peaches

Peaches

Yield: 5 quarts

10 lbs. peaches, Alberta are best
1½ qts. water
1¾ cups honey

Dip the peaches in boiling water for 1 minute, then into cold water. It is helpful to have a stainless steel rack or basket for this purpose. Peel and pit. Cut in halves or quarters, as desired, and treat to prevent darkening. To prepare the syrup, heat the water and honey to a boil until honey is dissolved. Pack the peaches into jars cavity-side down, overlapping the layers. Pack to within ½-inch from top of jars. Pour boiling syrup to the same level. Complete seals. Process for 30 minutes in a boiling-water bath.

Pineapple

Yield: 4 pints

8 cups pineapple (about 3 large)
4 cups water
1½ cups honey

Cut the pineapple into desired shapes. Prepare the syrup by adding honey to water and heating. Add the pineapple and simmer 3-5 minutes. Pack into hot sterilized jars. Complete seals. Process for 15 minutes in a boiling-water bath.

Pineapple may also be packed in its own juice. Put the cut pineapple into a pan with ¼ cup water. Begin to heat until the juice begins to flow. Pack into hot sterilized jars. Complete seals. Process for 15 minutes in a boiling-water bath.

Honey Pears

Yield: 7 quarts

50 medium size pears, Bartlett are best
2 qts. water
3 cups honey

Wash pears. Core and peel; cut into halves or quarters. To prevent browning of fruit before cooking, dip them in a solution of 2 tablespoons salt, 2 tablespoons vinegar, and 1 gallon water as you are peeling and coring. Rinse well in cold water. Be sure that the pears are firm and not overripe. Make the syrup mixture and heat in a large pot. Add the pears; cook for 6 minutes. Pack into sterilized jars and cover with syrup to within ½-inch from tops. Complete seals. Process for 25 minutes in a boiling-water bath.

Pears should be picked or bought while still slightly green and spread out in a cool place to ripen. This usually takes about 3 days. During this ripening process they are turning to sugar. Pears tend to be too soft for canning if they are tree ripened. Try to use evenly ripe pears for each batch.

For cinnamon pears, add 4-5 cinnamon sticks while cooking the syrup mixture. Remove the sticks before packing.

Minted Pears

Yield: 7 pints

7 lbs. pears
⅔ cup green creme de menthe

Prepare 4¾ cups light syrup (see p. 93) in a large kettle and keep hot but not boiling. Wash, peel, halve, and core the pears. Treat for darkening as for Honey Pears. Stir the creme de menthe into the syrup. Add pears and heat 2-3 minutes. Pack hot pears into hot sterilized jars, overlapping the center cavities. Leave ½-inch of headspace. Cover with hot syrup to the same level. Complete seals. Process in a boiling-water bath 25 minutes for pints, 30 minutes for quarts.

Plums

Yield: 4 pints

4 lbs. plums, the firmer varieties are best
2 cups honey
4 cups water

Wash plums. Prick with a sterilized pin to prevent the fruit from bursting while cooking. Prepare the syrup and heat to a boil. Add the plums and cook for 2 minutes. Remove from heat, cover, and let stand for 30 minutes. Pack plums into sterilized jars. Cover with the boiling syrup to within ½-inch from tops. Complete seals. Process for 20 minutes in a boiling-water bath.

Preserved Whole Persimmons

persimmons
honey

Wash and remove stem area from the fruit. Put a thin layer of honey in the bottom of hot sterilized jars. Add a layer of whole ripe persimmons, then another layer of honey. Repeat layers until jar is full to within ½-inch of top. Fruit should be firmly packed. The honey and persimmon juice will mix together to form a syrup. Complete seals and process in a boiling-water bath, pints for 15 minutes, quarts for 20 minutes.

Rhubarb

Yield: 4 pints

8 cups rhubarb
2 cups honey

Wash the rhubarb stalks. Cut into 1-inch pieces. Pour the honey over the rhubarb pieces. Let stand for 4 hours. Heat slowly to a boil. Pack into hot sterilized jars to within ½-inch from tops. Complete seals. Process for 10 minutes in a boiling-water bath.

Tomato Sauce

Yield: 9 pints

8 quarts tomatoes, peeled and chopped
2 cups chopped green peppers
2 cups chopped onions
⅓ cup honey
1 cup vinegar
2 teaspoons salt
3 teaspoons ground cinnamon
2 teaspoons ground cloves
3 teaspoons allspice

Wash tomatoes. Dip into boiling water for 1 minute to loosen the skins. Plunge into cold water and slip off the skins. Chop tomatoes and put in a large pot; add the peppers, onion, honey, and vinegar. Bring to a boil and simmer slowly for 4 hours. Add the spices during the last 15 minutes. Spoon hot into hot sterilized jars to within ½-inch of the tops. Complete seals. Process in a boiling-water bath for 45 minutes.

This sauce is also delicious without the spices.

Hot Sauce

Yield: 9 pints

12 pounds tomatoes
2 stalks celery, chopped
2½ cups chopped onion
3 hot peppers, chopped
6 inches of stick cinnamon
1½ teaspoons ground cloves
1 tablespoon dry mustard
½ cup honey
2 cups vinegar
¼ cup salt

Peel tomatoes. Cook for 15 minutes, then drain half of the juice (leaving about 6 cups). Reserve the drained liquid for drinking or cooking. Add the celery, onion and peppers to the tomatoes and simmer for 1½ hours. Tie the cinnamon sticks in cheesecloth; add it along with the remaining ingredients and continue cooking for 1½ hours more. Remove the cinnamon. Pack sauce into hot jars to within ½-inch of the tops. Complete seals. Process for 5 minutes in a boiling-water bath.

California-style Hot Sauce

Yield: 7 pints

3½ quarts tomatoes, peeled = 10 cups
6 jalapeños—or more if you like it HOT
6 sweet banana peppers
2 large bell peppers
2 medium size onions

After peeling the tomatoes, put them in a large pot and cook down for ½ hour. Chop the peppers and onions. For a milder sauce, remove the seeds from the jalapeños. (With jalapeños it's a good idea to wear rubber gloves, as these peppers will burn your hands.) Add the peppers and onions to the tomatoes and simmer for 1 hour. Pack into hot sterilized jars to within ½-inch of the tops. Complete seals. Process for 5 minutes in a boiling-water bath.

Hot Salsa

Yield: 6 pints

5 pounds ripe tomatoes = 2 quarts peeled
2 pound hot chiles (long green chiles)
1 pound onions
2 teaspoons salt
½ teaspoon black pepper
⅓ cup lemon juice

Peel and chop the tomatoes into small pieces. Chop the onions. To remove the skins from the chiles, place them under the broiler to crisp the skins. Allow to cool, then peel off the skins. Chop into small pieces. Combine all ingredients and bring to a boil. Pack into hot sterilized jars. Complete seals. Process for 5 minutes in a boiling-water bath.

Green tomatoes may also be used for equally delicious results. Also, you may include 3 small jalapeños, chopped, for a hotter sauce.

Tomato Paste

Yield: 8 half-pints

8 quarts peeled and chopped tomatoes
1½ cups chopped bell peppers
2 bay leaves
1 tablespoon salt
2 cloves garlic

Combine the tomatoes, peppers, bay leaves, and salt. Bring to a boil and cook slowly for 1 hour. Press through a fine sieve. Return to the pot and add the pressed garlic. Continue cooking slowly until thick, about 2½ hours. Pour into hot sterilized jars to within ¼-inch of the top. Complete seals. Process in a boiling-water bath for 45 minutes.

Seasoned Tomato Puree

Yield: 7 quarts

12 quarts tomatoes
9 cups chopped onions
6 cups chopped carrots
6 cups chopped celery
4½ cups chopped green peppers
2 tablespoons salt
garlic
basil
oregano

Wash the tomatoes and dip into boiling water for 1 minute to loosen the skins. Plunge into cold water. Slip off the skins. Put in a large pot and combine with the onions, carrots, celery, and green peppers. Cook until tender, about 30 minutes. Press through a fine sieve. Add the garlic and salt; cook for 1½ hours, until thick. Add the spices during the last 15 minutes of cooking. Pour hot into hot sterilized jars to within ¼-inch of the tops. Complete seals. Process in a boiling-water bath for 45 minutes.

Tomato Chutney

Yield: 6 pints

16 large ripe tomatoes
3 large apples
3 large pears
3 large peaches
2 onions, chopped
1 cup apple cider vinegar
1½ cups honey
1 tablespoon salt
½ cup mixed pickling spices

Plunge tomatoes, apples, pears, and peaches into boiling water, then immerse in cold water. Core and peel, then chop fine. Mix all the ingredients together and boil until thick. Spoon hot mixture into hot sterilized jars to within ½-inch of the tops. Complete seals. Process in a boiling-water bath for 5 minutes.

Canned Whole Tomatoes

Cold Pack

Italian pear-shaped tomatoes are the best variety for canning since they have very few seeds; however, any variety will do.

2½ pounds tomatoes per quart
1 teaspoon salt per quart
2 teaspoons vinegar or lemon juice per quart

Scald tomatoes in boiling water, then immerse them in cold water. Core and peel (first cut out the core then slip off the skin, as this order is easier). Keep tomatoes and their juice together, add no water. Pack into hot quart jars, smashing down the tomatoes after every 3 or 4 to release the air. Pack to within ½-inch of the top of the jar. Insert a clean knife down the sides of the jar to release air bubbles. Add the salt and vinegar or lemon juice, clean the rim of the jar, and complete the seal. Process in a boiling-water bath for 50 minutes.

Canned Tomatoes

Hot Pack

2½ pounds tomatoes per quart
1 teaspoon salt per quart
2 teaspoons vinegar or lemon juice per quart

Scald tomatoes in boiling water, then immerse them in cold water. Core and peel (first cut out the core, then slip off the skin). Put the tomatoes into a pan with the salt and vinegar or lemon juice. Bring to a boil and boil for 5 minutes, stirring constantly. Spoon hot into hot sterilized jars to within ½-inch of the tops. Complete seals. Process in a boiling-water bath for 15 minutes.

Stewed Tomatoes

Yield: 6 quarts

6 quarts tomatoes
¾ cup chopped green peppers
¾ cup chopped onions
1 cup chopped celery
2 tablespoons celery salt
2 tablespoons honey

Wash the tomatoes. Dip into boiling water for 1 minute to loosen the skins, then plunge into cold water. Skin and cut into chunks. Mix all the ingredients together and heat just enough to dissolve the honey. Pack into sterilized jars to within ½-inch of the tops. Complete seals. Process in a boiling-water bath for 55 minutes.

Outrageous Tomato Soup

Yield: 9 quarts (18 pints)

12 quarts tomatoes (20 pounds)
6 tablespoons arrowroot
  or 12 tablespoons flour
14 tablespoons butter or oil
3 tablespoons vegetable salt
6 medium onions   1 stalk celery
14 sprigs fresh parsley   3 bay leaves
6 tablespoons honey   2 teaspoons pepper

Wash and cut up the tomatoes. Chop the onions, celery, parsley, and bay leaves. Add this to the tomatoes and cook until the celery is tender. Put through a sieve to remove the tomato peels. Mix the arrowroot or flour with the melted butter to a smooth paste. Thin with some of the tomato mixture.

Add this to the boiling soup; stir in well. Add the honey, salt and pepper; add remaining spices during the last 15 minutes of cooking. If a smoother consistency is desired, put through a sieve again. Pack hot soup into hot sterilized jars to within ½-inch of the tops. Complete seals. Process 15 minutes in a boiling-water bath.

Tomato Soup

Yield: 9 quarts

12 quarts tomatoes (20 pounds)
6 tablespoons arrowroot
 or 14 tablespoons flour
14 tablespoons butter or oil
6 medium onions   4 bell peppers
4 large carrots   4 stalks celery
14 sprigs fresh parsley   3 bay leaves
3 teaspoons salt   6 tablespoons honey
2 teaspoons pepper

Wash and cut the tomatoes. Chop the onions, celery, parsley, and bay leaves. Add this to the tomatoes and cook until the celery is tender. Put through a sieve to remove the tomato peels. Mix the arrowroot or flour with the melted butter to a smooth paste. Thin with some of the tomato mixture. Add this to the boiling soup; stir in well. Add the honey, salt, and pepper; add remaining spices during the last 15 minutes of cooking. If a smoother consistency is desired, put through a sieve again. Pack hot soup into hot sterilized jars to within ½-inch of the tops. Complete seals. Process for 15 minutes in a boiling-water bath.

Apple-Cherry Juice

Yield: 3-4 pints

3 pounds apples
1¼ pounds cherries
3 cups water
⅓ cup honey

Wash and core apples. Wash and pit cherries. If a juicer is available, juice the fruit. Otherwise, grind apples and cherries through a food chopper or chop finely. Bring fruit and water to a boil in a 4-6 quart kettle. Reduce heat and cook slowly for about 10 minutes. Strain through a cloth bag. Let fruit juice stand 1 to 2 hours to let sediment settle, if desired. Add honey to juice and heat throughly. Pour hot juice into hot sterilized jars to within ½-inch of tops. Complete seals. Process in hot-water bath for 15 minutes.

Pineapple-Grapefruit Juice

Yield: 4-5 pints

2 large pineapples
6 large grapefruits

Remove crowns from pineapples, peel, quarter, and core. If a juicer is available, juice the fruit. Otherwise grind through a food chopper using a fine blade or chop finely. In a medium saucepan bring pineapple to a boil, reduce heat, and simmer for 10 minutes. Strain through a cloth bag. You should have 3 cups of juice. Cut grapefruits in half and extract the juice. You should have 6 cups. Combine juices and bring to a boil. Pour hot juice into hot sterilized jars to within ½-inch of tops. Complete seals. Process in a hot-water bath for 20 minutes.

Strawberry Juice

Yield: 7 quarts

24 cups berries, stemmed and sliced
3 cups honey

If a juicer is available, juice the berries. Otherwise, they may be ground-up in a blender and put through a strainer. Heat juice and honey to a boil. Pack into hot sterilized jars to within ½-inch of tops. Process in a hot-water bath for 30 minutes.

For a strawberry lover, this juice is pure delight. It adds exciting flavor to apple juice when mixed 1 quart strawberry juice to 1 gallon apple juice.

Strawberry-Apple Juice

Follow the same procedure as for Apple-Cherry Juice using 1¼ pounds of strawberries. This juice is absolutely delicious!

Fruit Juices [except tomato]

Wash fruit and remove pits. If you have a juicer, juice the fruit. Otherwise, you can crush it and strain through a cloth bag. Fruits tend to be sweet enough as is, but if you want a sweeter product, add about ¾ cup honey to each gallon of juice. Heat to simmering—185°F to 210°F. Fill hot sterilized jars to ½-inch of the tops. Complete seals. Process pints or quarts in a hot-water bath for 15 minutes.

Tomato Juice

Use ripe, juicy tomatoes. Wash, remove stem ends, and cut into pieces. Juice them in a juicer or simmer until softened, stirring often, and put through a strainer. Add 1 teaspoon salt to each quart of juice. Reheat just to boiling. Fill hot sterilized jars with boiling hot juice to ½-inch of tops. Complete seals and process pints or quarts in a boiling-water bath for 10 minutes.

Chapter 4

Pickling

Pickling

Tangy, crisp, spiced pickles or relish add interest to any meal and play an important part in the digestive tract. Apple cider vinegar stimulates the flow of saliva and gastric juices, thus soothing the stomach. Wine and grain vinegars, which are not digestible, tend to be irritants to the stomach.

Pickles and Relishes

Pickle products are classified on the basis of the ingredients used as well as the method of preparation. There are four different kinds of pickled products: brined pickles, fresh-pack pickles, relishes, and fruit pickles. Many pickle recipes are quick and easy, not requiring the long fermenting of brined pickles.

Brined pickles go through a curing process of about three weeks. Brine draws the moisture and natural sugars from the foods and forms lactic acid to keep them from spoiling. Pickling cucumbers, green tomatoes, and cabbage are suitable for the brine method. Brined or fermented pickles are made in a low-salt brine and usually do not require desalting before they are used. Cucumbers, however, may be cured in a high-salt brine (10% salt) and should be soaked in water before further processing. Curing changes cucumber color from a bright green to a yellow green or olive color. The white interior of the cucumber becomes uniformly translucent. The final product is tender and firm, both inside and out. Good sauerkraut, or brined cabbage, has a pleasant, tart and tangy flavor. The color is a creamy white, while the texture is crisp and firm. The shreds should be uniformly cut, about the thinness of a dime. Sauerkraut is high in Vitamin C because the fermentation process causes little loss of this vitamin. Sauerkraut, like yogurt, has a high lactic acid content which aids digestion by helping to stimulate the growth of beneficial bacteria in the digestive tract.

Fresh-pack pickles are easy to prepare and allow much diversity in flavor. They are usually soaked in a low-salt brine for several hours or overnight, then drained and processed with vinegar, herbs, and spices. Produce suitable for fresh-pack pickles includes cucumbers (whole or sliced), green beans, mushrooms, and mixed vegetables.

Relishes are prepared from a combination of fruits and vegetables which are chopped, seasoned, and then cooked. Bright color and uniformity in size of pieces make for an attractive product. Relishes accent the flavor of other foods, being either hot and spicy or sweet and spicy. Products classified as relishes include chutneys, piccalilli, horseradish, catsup, chow chow, and corn relish. Chutney is oriental in origin and is eaten as a condiment. Basically a mixture of chopped fruits, vegetables, nuts, and berries, a chutney may be hotly seasoned or sweetly spiced. Picalilli is a combination of salted fruits or vegetables and spices and vinegar. It was considered to be one of the Seven Sours by the old Pennsylvania Dutch. Horseradish is a hot relish made from the ground root of the fresh horseradish plant. Catsup is traditionally made with tomatoes combined with chopped vegetables and enlivened by the addition of salt, pepper, and spices. The mixture is boiled down to make it naturally thick and highly concentrated. A chow chow is characteristically hot and sour. It is made from finely diced fruits and vegetables mixed with spices and hot pepper. Corn relish is sweet and tart and is made from corn combined with small amounts of other vegetables and spices. Varied in name, all these products add a special quality to a meal.

Fruit pickles are made from fruits which have been simmered in a spicy, sweet-sour syrup. Peaches, pears, and watermelon rind are among the most common fruit pickles. Fruit pickles go well with other foods but can be special treats all by themselves.

Selection of Ingredients

Choose food for pickling that is firm, fresh, and free from bruises or blemishes. Use the fruits and vegetables as soon as possible after picking. Refrigerate the cucumbers if they cannot be used within 24 hours of picking, as they deteriorate rapidly at room temperature. It is best to use fruit that is slightly underripe, as it holds its shape better. The vegetables should be nearly the same size, so they cook at the same rate. All produce should be free from spoilage or mold spots. Although processing will kill any spores, it won't help the off-flavor that develops from the spoiled areas.

Delicious pickles can be obtained from zucchini and yellow squash, as well as from pickling cucumbers. Small or medium cucumbers or squash may be pickled whole; larger vegetables should be cut into chunks or chips. Mixed pickles made from cauliflower, onions, carrots, and beans offer a great pickle plate.

Pure sea salt or "pickling salt" is best for pickling. Table salt usually has chemicals added to prevent lumping which may interfere with best results by causing some cloudiness or darkening.

Use a good cider vinegar for pickling, 4 to 6 percent acetic acid. Cider vinegar may slightly darken some foods but is preferable for its digestibility, flavor, and aroma. If the vinegar contains much sediment, strain it before use to avoid a cloudy product. Pickled products, normally on the low-end of the pH scale, require acidity to make them safe from botulism poisoning. Therefore, to prevent loss of acetic acid, avoid long boiling of the vinegar solution.

Fresh, whole spices produce the best flavor. Ground spices will cloud the pickled product and alter the desired flavor. If the spices are to be removed before packing, tie them in a square of cheesecloth. Pickling spices usually include whole cloves, peppercorns, stick cinnamon, mace, dill, tiny red peppers, mustard seed, allspice, bay leaves, and ginger root.

Water containing high concentrations of iron may cause darkening of the pickles. Otherwise, it makes little difference whether soft or hard water is used.

Do not use alum. The most common form of alum is potassium aluminum sulfate which may cause digestive disturbance. Alum is not necessary to make pickles crisp and firm when good methods and fresh ingredients are used; in fact, alum may soften pickles if used incorrectly. Although fresh ingredients should produce a good product, a grape leaf added to each jar will ensure crispness.

Packing Pickled Foods

Wash the vegetables thoroughly in cold water with a soft vegetable brush or your hands. Be careful not to bruise them, but wash and rinse well. It is important to remove all traces of soil which could cause bacterial action. Discard any mold-damaged areas and spoiled fruit or vegetables.

Prepare the product and fill the jars as recommended in the recipes, leaving the necessary headroom. Avoid packing so tightly that the brine or syrup is prevented from filling the spaces around and over the product. Each recipe contains specific packing instructions, since pickle and relish recipes differ slightly. Pickled foods should be processed in a boiling-water bath.

Pickled products should be stored in a cool, dry, dark place, as recommended for other canned goods. When a jar is opened, always look for the usual signs of spoilage. In addition, be alert for unusual softness, mushiness, or slipperiness, and discard any products that have developed any of these signs of spoilage.

The mild taste of a fresh cucumber and the tangy flavor of a good pickle are distinct and different experiences. Pickling is a way to enjoy the greatest variety from your garden's yield.

Equipment

An important item in pickle-making is a crock, used for fermenting or brining. A large glass jar or unchipped enamelware pot is also suitable for this purpose. A large kettle is needed for cooking the ingredients. The utensils should be stainless steel, enamelware, glass or wood. Avoid copper utensils, as they turn pickles a peculiar shade of green; cast iron may turn them black. The action of acetic acid or salt with galvanized steel utensils may develop a poisonous substance. Always avoid aluminum utensils: aluminum is an unstable metal which reacts with foods altering their flavor and color.

Helpful Hints

1. Jars for pickles should never have held any oily substance.

2. Horseradish helps to keep pickles and vinegar clear. Put fresh sliced horse-radish root into pickles that have already been skimmed. Any remaining scum will be carried to the bottom as the horseradish sinks, leaving the vinegar clear.

3. A cluster or two of green grapes added to the brine will preserve the strength of the vinegar.

4. Mustard seed will prevent mold from forming in the vinegar.

5. To keep a barrel of pickles firm, add ½ bushel of grape leaves to a pickle brine.

6. Tough, shriveled pickles are the result of too much salt, too sweet a pickling solution, or too strong a vinegar. Allowing too much time to elapse between gathering and pickling may also cause shriveling.

7. Soft pickles are the result of too strong a vinegar or too weak a brine.

8. Hollow pickles are caused by using imperfect cucumbers or allowing too much time to lapse between picking and pickling.

9. Slippery pickles are the result of the cucumbers standing above the brine, too weak a brine solution, or the presence of scum in the crock. Pickles stored in too warm an area will also be soft and slippery. Slippery pickles should not be eaten.

10. Dark pickles are the result of too much iron in the water or the use of iron utensils. Using ground spices or cooking the pickles too long with the spices will also cause darkening.

11. A white sediment in the bottom of the jar may be the result of impure salt.

12. Always cut the cucumbers from the vine and leave a short bit of stem. Cucumbers pulled from the vine may rot if the flesh is injured, or the vines themselves may be injured by yanking. Remove the blossom end since any enzymes located here can cause softening during brining.

13. When purchasing a used stoneware crock, check its inside. If the crock has been used to preserve eggs in a solution of water glass, it will have a whitish stain. In this case, the crock should not be used for making pickles. (Water glass is either sodium silicate or potassium silicate which has been dissolved in water to form a colorless, syrupy liquid for preserving eggs.)

Pickling Spice

Use only whole spices. Measure by weight (ounces). Mix equal amounts by weight:

Allspice   Whole cloves
Bay leaves, crumbled   Coriander
Black peppercorns   Ginger root
Cardamom   Mace
Celery seeds   Mustard seeds
Cinnamon stick, broken   Red chilis, crumbled

Commercial Pickle Sizes

Name	Length in Inches	Count per Quart
Midgets No. 1	1¼-2	162
Midgets No. 2	1¼-2	112
Midgets No. 3	1¼-2	85
Gherkins No. 1	2-2¾	65
Gherkins No. 2	2-2¾	56
Gherkins No. 3	2-2¾	40
Medium	3-4	10-30
Large	4 & over	3-10

Vinegar

Homemade vinegars are fairly easy to make. The acid strength, however, can vary greatly. Vinegar suitable for pickling brines must be between 4 and 6 percent acid strength (40 to 60 grain). Homemade vinegar should be tested for acid strength. (The necessary supplies can be found at a chemical supply house.) The correct acid strength is very important for obtaining consistent quality in pickling. The surest way to have the correct acid strength is to rely on commercially prepared vinegars saving your delicious homemade vinegar for salads and other cooking purposes.

Apple Cider Vinegar

To juice your own apples, cut them into small pieces without peeling. Add water to cover and simmer for 40 minutes. Press through a jelly bag, then strain the juice through a flannel bag. Commercial apple juice may also be used. The juice should be strained through several layers of cheesecloth to remove any sediment. Pour the strained juice into a clean crock, watertight wooden barrel, or dark-colored glass jugs. Leave a headspace of about 20% of the container size as the juice does expand during fermentation. Cover the container with several layers of cheesecloth or a piece of muslin. This allows the air in, but keeps the dust and insects out. Store the container in a cold, dark place. Fermentation will take from 4 to 6 months. Check the vinegar after 4 months. If it is not strong enough for your taste, replace the cheesecloth and let it work longer. When the vinegar is strong enough, strain the scum layer from the surface (this is the "mother"—save it to use as a starter for your next batch of vinegar). Then strain the vinegar through several layers of cheesecloth to remove any additional residue. Pour the vinegar into bottles, and seal.

Subsequent batches of vinegar can be started by adding the "mother" to the apple juice. The fermentation time will be shorter for these batches.

Herb Vinegars

To make an herb vinegar, you simply add fresh herbs to your finished product. Add about 3 sprigs of fresh herbs to each quart. Some popular flavors are: Tarragon, Basil-Tarragon, Basil-Garlic, and Garlic (about 3 peeled and sliced cloves per quart).

Honey Vinegar

Mix together 1 qt. of filtered honey and 8 qts. of warm water. Allow the mixture to stand in a warm place until fermentation ceases (about two months). The vinegar should be clear in color. Test for acid strength. When strong enough, strain and seal in clean sterilized jars.

This vinegar is excellent to use for Herb Vinegars.

Molasses Vinegar

1 gallon molasses
4½ gallons water

Mix molasses and water thoroughly. Pour into a crock, allowing 20% headspace. Cover crock with several layers of cheesecloth. Place where it is 70°-90° F and light. Let work for 2 months and test. When strong enough, strain and bottle.

Spiced Vinegars

1 qt. vinegar
1 cup honey
5 inches of stick cinnamon
1 teaspoon allspice
1 tablespoon mustard seed
1 teaspoon whole cloves
1 teaspoon salt

Tie the whole spices in a cheesecloth. Mix all ingredients together, heating if necessary to dissolve the honey. Remove the spice bag and bottle the vinegar.

Brined Pickles

In the brine method of preserving foods, vegetables (such as cucumbers or cabbage) are dropped into an 8-10% salt solution. The salt helps convert the natural sugars in the vegetables into lactic acid during the fermentation process. It is important to maintain conditions that encourage the growth of lactic acid bacteria and to prevent the growth of other organisms that may cause spoilage. Lactic acid is a critical element in maintaining proper nutrition. This substance aids digestion and helps to destroy harmful bacteria in the digestive tract.

For success in fermenting pickles or sauerkraut, it is important to pack the vegetables securely in a crock that will keep the air out during all stages of processing and thus prevent the growth of spoilage organisms. The temperature of the vegetables and brine should be between 70° to 80°F. If it is too warm, fermentation will occur too rapidly and an inferior product will result.

It is also important to "scum" the crock during the fermentation process. Scum forms if the container cannot be sealed tightly and air is present. This indicates the growth of spoilage organisms. If allowed to continue growing, the scum will destroy the acid balance in the crock and promote the growth of spoilage organisms. This will ruin the batch of pickles.

To further crisp your pickles, add a handful of grape leaves (rather than alum) during the brining process.

Brine Pickles

Yield: 18 quarts

15 lbs. small cucumbers
2 cups salt per gallon of water
5 gallon crock
salt

Carefully wash the cucumbers and remove the stem ends. Pack the cucumbers into a stoneware crock. Cover with a brine made by dissolving 2 cups of salt to 1 gallon of water (you should need about 4 gallons of brine: 8 cups salt to 4 gallons water). Fill with enough brine to *cover* the cucumbers. Cover the crock with a plate or wax-covered board. The "cover" should be wrapped with cheesecloth or muslin, and it should fit snugly *inside* the rim of the crock. The "cover" should then be weighted down with a clean jar filled with water, which will keep the cucumbers pushed down under the brine.

The next day add 3 cups of salt to the top of the plate. Salt added below the plate may sink, causing the salt solution to be very strong at the bottom but so weak at the surface that the pickles may spoil. The purpose of this additional salt is to maintain a 10% brine solution. Brine in which a fresh egg floats is approximately 10%.

At the end of 1 week, remove the weight and cover. Skim the brine with a spoon if any scum has formed. Wipe around the rim of the crock at the surface of the liquid with a clean, damp cloth. Wash the cover. Rewrap the cover with a clean piece of cheesecloth or muslin, replace it and weight it down. Add ¾ cup of salt to the top of the plate.

Always remove scum as it forms. It is important to check this every day.

At the end of each week, repeat the cleaning procedure and add ¾ cup of salt to the top of the plate. Remember to skim the surface if necessary. The vegetables should always be completely covered with brine.

Fermentation should be complete in 4-6 weeks. Test this by tapping the crock firmly on its side. If no bubbles form, the fermentation is complete. The cucumbers should be a dark olive-green color throughout with no white spots.

When the fermenting is complete, the pickles may be eaten from the crock. They may also be further seasoned and packed in jars for future use. Before packing these brined cucumbers in jars, soak them in water to remove the salt. Use 3 times as much cold water as cucumbers and change the water every eight hours. Stir cucumbers occasionally. The salt should be removed after 24 hours.

After desalting, immediately pack cucumbers into clean sterilized quart jars. You may use one of the following recipes:

Kosher Pickles

To each jar of brined cucumbers add:

1 clove garlic, sliced
1 bay leaf
½ teaspoon mustard seed
1 piece red hot pepper

Dill Pickles

To each jar of brined cucumbers add:

2 heads fresh dill
2 cloves garlic, sliced
½ teaspoon mustard seed

For either recipe, cover cucumbers with the following brine:

2¼ cups salt
3 cups vinegar
12 quarts water

Bring to a boil and pour over cucumbers to within ¼-inch of top of jar. Complete seals. Process for 15 minutes in a boiling-water bath.

Sauerkraut

Sauerkraut is an important winter source of vitamin C. It is also important to our diets because of its high lactic acid content. When making sauerkraut, no water need be added to make a brine; the salt will drain sufficient moisture from the cabbage.

Yield: 16 quarts

50 lbs. cabbage
1 lb. salt (1½ cups)
large crock (about 10 gallon size, or
* 2 five gallon crocks)*

Use only firm, mature heads of cabbage. Remove the outer leaves and the core. Use a shredder or sharp knife to cut the cabbage into shreds about the thickness of a dime.

In a large container, mix 3 tablespoons of salt with 5 pounds of shredded cabbage. Let the salted cabbage stand for several minutes to wilt slightly; this will allow packing without excessive breaking or bruising of the shreds.

Pack salted cabbage firmly and evenly into a large, clean crock. Using a large wooden spoon, or your hands, press the cabbage down firmly until the juice comes to the surface. Repeat the shredding, salting and packing of cabbage until the crock is filled to within 3 or 4 inches of the top.

Cover the cabbage with a clean, thin, white cloth, such as muslin. Tuck the edges down against the inside of the crock and cover with a plate or a round paraffined board that just fits inside the crock, so that the cabbage is not exposed to the air. Put a weight, such as a clean rock, or a glass jar filled with water, on top of the plate so that the brine comes to the plate but not over it. The amount of water in the glass jar can be adjusted to give just enough pressure to keep the fermenting cabbage covered with brine.

Formation of gas bubbles indicates that fermentation is taking place. A room temperature of 68° to 72° is best for fermenting cabbage. Fermentation is usually complete in 3-6 weeks. Larger batches require a longer fermentation time. When bubbling stops, the sauerkraut is ready.

Each day remove the scum from the top of the brine by skimming carefully, then replace the scummy cloth with a clean, sterile one. Wash and scald the plate before returning it to the top of the crock. If you don't skim your fermenting product, the scum will weaken the acid-content and turn your produce into a dark, mushy mess. The brine may get slimy if the weather is too warm. If this occurs, discard the batch and wait until cooler weather.

To store sauerkraut, heat it to a simmer but do not boil, and pack hot into hot sterilized jars, covering with the juice to within ½-inch from the top of jar. Complete seals. Process quarts for 20 minutes or pints for 15 minutes in a boiling-water bath.

As a variation, you may spice your sauerkraut when packing with a bit of caraway seed or dill seed. Onion rings and garlic cloves are also good additions.

Marinated Olives

Pick the olives when they turn dark around late November. Make four even cuts from top to bottom of each olive and soak them in cold water. Change the water at least once a day, twice if possible. After 15 days, taste the olives. If the taste is mild, and the bitterness gone, it is time to marinate them. Make a marinade in the following ratio:

1 cup oil
1 cup vinegar
12 cloves garlic, chopped
1 teaspoon oregano

Pack the olives in clean, sterilized quart jars. Cover with the marinade and seal. *Keep refrigerated.* They are ready to eat after one week.

Marinated olives have a refrigerated "shelf life" of two months—about the same as any opened, refrigerated jar or can of olives. For longer storage, process in a pressure canner for 60 minutes at 240°F, 10 pounds pressure.

Canning Olives

Olives are a low-acid food. This means they are susceptible to clostridium botulinum. For protection most preparations of olives require processing in a pressure canner. Marinated olives are easy to prepare and their storage in vinegar increases their pH level making them less susceptible to spoilage.

For other olive recipes and more information on the dangers of home canning olives, write to: Cooperative Extension, University of California, Davis, California 95616; Bulletin HXT-29, Home Pickling of Olives.

Bread and Butter Cubes

Yield: 4 pints

24 small cucumbers, cubed
8 medium-sized onions, sliced
4 three-inch cinnamon sticks
2 teaspoons whole allspice
3 teaspoons mustard seeds   ½ cup salt
1 teaspoon turmeric   ¼ teaspoon cayenne
1 teaspoon celery seed   1¼ cups honey

In glass containers, layer the cucumbers and onions, sprinkling salt between layers. Cover and let stand overnight. Drain thoroughly and rinse with cold water, then drain again. Mix the honey and vinegar together in a large kettle and begin to heat slowly. Tie cinnamon and allspice together in a square of cheesecloth, add to the vinegar and boil for 1 minute. Stir in the remaining spices. Add the cucumbers and onions and heat for 25 minutes over a low heat. Remove spice bag. Pack into hot sterilized jars to within ½-inch from top. Complete seals and process for 10 minutes in a boiling-water bath.

Bread and Butter Pickles

Yield: 8 pints

30 four or five inch cucumbers, sliced
10 medium onions, sliced
4 teaspoons salt

Sprinkle cucumbers and onions with salt. Let stand one hour and drain thoroughly.

5 cups apple cidar vinegar
2 teaspoons celery seeds
2 teaspoons ground ginger
2 cups honey
1 teaspoon turmeric
2 teaspoons mustard seed

Make brine of the above ingredients and bring to a boil. Add the cucumbers and onions; bring them to a boiling point and simmer for 8 minutes. Pack into jars to within ½-inch from tops. Complete seals and process for 10 minutes in a boiling-water bath.

Dilled Green Beans

Yield: 4 pints

2 lbs. green beans
2 teaspoons cayenne
4 cloves garlic
4 heads of dill
2½ cups water
2½ cups vinegar
¼ cup salt

Pack the beans lengthwise into sterilized jars leaving ¼-inch headroom. To each jar add ½ teaspoon cayenne, 1 clove garlic, sliced, and 1 head of fresh dill. Combine the water, salt, and vinegar and heat to a boil. Pour over the beans to within ½-inch from tops of jars. Complete seals and process for 10 minutes in a boiling-water bath.

Dilled Small Green Tomatoes

Yield: 6 quarts

24 cups small green firm tomatoes
6 cloves garlic, peeled
6 stalks celery, cut in 2-inch lengths
6 green bell peppers, quartered
8 cups water
4 cups vinegar
1 cup sea salt
6 heads fresh dill

Make a brine of the water, vinegar, and salt. Boil with the dill for 5 minutes. Keep hot until needed. Wash the tomatoes and pack into hot sterilized jars. Add to each jar 1 clove garlic, 1 stalk celery, cut in 2-inch lengths, and 1 quartered green pepper. Pour the hot brine over the contents of the jars to within ½-inch of the tops. Complete seals. Process for 5 minutes in a boiling-water bath. These will be ready for use in 4-6 weeks. Makes a delicious condiment for a curry dinner.

Grape Leaves

Yield: 4 pints

200 whole, medium sized grape leaves
4 teaspoons salt
2 qts. water
2 cups lemon juice

Add salt to 2 quarts of water and bring to a boil. Add the grape leaves about 25 at a time and cook for 30 seconds. Drain. Form into loose rolls and pack vertically into pint jars. Add lemon juice to 2 qts. of fresh water. Bring to a boil. Pour over the grape leaves to within ½-inch from the tops of the jars. Complete seals and process for 15 minutes in a boiling-water bath.

Green Tomato Pickles

Yield: 4 pints

2 qts. medium-sized green tomatoes
3 tablespoons salt
2 cups cider vinegar
½ cup honey
3 tablespoons mustard seed
½ teaspoon celery seeds
½ teaspoon turmeric
3 large onions, thinly sliced
2 sweet bell peppers (red) thinly sliced
1 tablespoon minced hot red pepper

Remove the stem end from the tomatoes and slice them about ½-inch thick. Toss with the salt and let stand in a glass or enamel container for 12 hours. Drain. Heat the vinegar, honey, and spices to a boil. Add the onions and simmer for 3 minutes. Add the tomatoes and peppers and simmer for 5 minutes longer, stirring gently occasionally. Pack into hot sterilized jars to within ½-inch from tops. Complete seals and process for 5 minutes in a boiling-water bath.

Homemade "Capers"

Yield: 2 half-pints

2 cups fresh green nasturtium seeds
¾ cup water
¼ cup salt
½ cup honey
1 cup cider vinegar

Wash and drain seeds. Mix water and salt together. Place seeds in a jar and pour liquid over. Cover and allow to stand for 48 hours. Drain seeds and pour them into sterilized half-pint jars. Heat the honey and vinegar just to boiling, stirring often to mix. Pour over seeds to within ½-inch of tops of jars. Complete seals and process for 5 minutes in a boiling-water bath.

This is an excellent addition to sauces or to salads. The flowers are easy to grow; their leaves contain large amounts of vitamin C and are delicious in salads. The flowers are also good on sandwiches or in soup.

Kosher-style Dill Pickles

Yield: 7 quarts

80 small cucumbers (about 3 inches long)
7 cups apple cider vinegar
7 cups water
14 tablespoons salt
fresh dill weed, 2 heads per qt.
garlic, 2 cloves per qt.
mustard seed, ½ teaspoon per qt.

Wash the cucumbers, scrubbing lightly with a vegetable brush. Make a brine of the vinegar, water, and salt and bring to a boil. Place a generous layer of dill, 2 cloves of sliced garlic, and ½ teaspoon mustard seed in the bottom of each clean sterilized jar. Pack cucumbers into the jars. When half full of cucumbers, add more dill. Complete packing. Fill the jars to within ½-inch from tops with the boiling brine. Complete seals and process for 20 minutes in a boiling-water bath.

Mixed Mustard Pickles

Yield: 6 pints

4 cups sliced green tomatoes
4 cups sliced string beans
4 cups small onions, peeled and sliced
1 large cauliflower, broken into flowerets
10 medium-sized cucumbers, sliced
¾ cup salt
½ lb. dry ground mustard
3 tablespoons cornstarch
 or 1 tablespoon arrowroot
¾ cup water   1 teaspoon turmeric
6 cups vinegar   1½ cups honey

Combine all vegetables in a large kettle, sprinkling each layer with salt. Cover and let stand overnight then drain thoroughly. Set aside. Mix together mustard, cornstarch (or arrowroot), water, and turmeric. Heat to a boil, stirring often. When dissolved, pour over vegetables, heat slowly to a boil, and boil gently for 15 minutes. Remove from heat for a few minutes. Stir, then reheat to a boil and cook 10 minutes longer. Spoon hot into hot sterilized jars to within ½-inch from tops. Complete seals and process for 10 minutes in a boiling-water bath.

Mustard Curry Pickles

Yield: 5 pints

24 cucumbers, about 4 inches long
½ cup salt
8 cups water
1½ teaspoons curry powder
2 cups apple cider vinegar
¼ cup mustard seed
1 tablespoon celery seed
1¾ cups honey

Wash cucumbers. Quarter them, or cut into thick slices. Combine with salt and water. Let stand for 5 hours then drain and rinse thoroughly. Pack the cucumbers into clean jars to within ½-inch from tops. Mix remaining ingredients in a pan, heat to a boil, and pour over the packed cucumbers. Complete seals and process for 5 minutes in a boiling-water bath.

These are easy to make and delicious with curry dishes.

Olive Oil Pickles

Yield: 6 pints

½ cup salt
12 cups sliced small cucumbers
3 cups water
4 tablespoons mustard seed
3 tablespoons celery seed
3 medium onions, sliced
2 qts. vinegar
¼ cup honey
⅔ cup olive oil

Layer the cucumbers and onions, sprinkling salt between the layers. Let stand 4 hours then drain, rinse with cold water, and drain again. Combine vinegar, water, and spices and bring to a boil. Add the drained vegetables and return to a boil. Remove from heat and stir in the honey and olive oil. Mix well. Return to a boil and pack into hot sterilized jars to within ¼-inch from tops. Complete seals and process for 10 minutes in a boiling-water bath.

Pickled Artichokes

Yield: 4 pints

48 small artichokes (3 inches in diameter)
 or 76 artichoke hearts
1 cup lemon juice
2 qts. water
vinegar
4 cups olive oil
4 cloves garlic
8 bay leaves
sweet basil
oregano

Pull off outer leaves. Cut off the top of the bud and trim the stem. Wash thoroughly. Mix the water and the lemon juice. Add the artichokes to this solution and bring to a boil. Simmer whole, small artichokes for 10 minutes, hearts for 3-5 minutes. Drain. Place the artichokes into clean pint jars, cover with vinegar and let stand overnight. Drain and cover with fresh vinegar. Let stand for an additional 4 hours, then drain again. Add to each jar: 1 whole clove of garlic, 2 bay leaves, ¼ teaspoon sweet basil and ¼ teaspoon oregano. Fill each jar with oil. Complete seals and process for 30 minutes in a boiling-water bath.

Pickled Beets

Yield: 6 pints

7½ lbs. beets (3 qts.)
4 cups apple cider vinegar
2 cups water

Wash and peel the beets and slice them into ¼-inch slices. Put water and vinegar in a saucepan and heat to a boil. Add the beets. Simmer for 15-20 minutes, until just tender. Pack the beets into hot sterilized jars to within ½-inch from tops. Pour the cooling liquid over the beets to just cover them. Complete seals and process for 30 minutes in a boiling-water bath.

French-style Pickled Beets

Yield: 6 pints

3 qts. beets
4 cups vinegar
mace
piece of ginger root
piece of horseradish

Wash the beets, and boil them until just tender. Plunge into cold water and slip off skins. Cut into slices or chunks. Tie spices in a piece of cheesecloth. Add to vinegar and slowly heat to a boil. Pack the beets into hot sterilized jars. Cover with the spiced vinegar to within ½-inch from tops. Complete seals. Process for 20 minutes in a boiling-water bath.

Pickled Carrot Sticks

Yield: 4 half-pints

1 lb. carrots, peeled
¼ cup honey
¾ cup vinegar
½ cup water
1 teaspoon mixed pickling spices

Slice the carrots into thin slices and steam for 5 minutes. Drain. Combine vinegar, water, honey, and spices in a medium-size saucepan. Bring to a boil, then simmer for 3 minutes. Pack the carrot sticks into hot sterilized jars. Cover with the hot liquid to within ½-inch from tops. Complete seals and process for 5 minutes in a boiling-water bath.

Pickled Crab Apples

Yield: 5 pints

7 lbs. crab apples
1 qt. vinegar
2 cups honey
3 teaspoons cinnamon
3 teaspoons cloves
3 teaspoons mace
3 teaspoons allspice

Apples should be of a uniform size. Do not pare them; just remove the stems. Make a syrup of the vinegar, honey, and spices. Heat just enough to dissolve the honey and cool. Add the crab apples to the syrup and heat slowly; heating too fast may burst the fruit. Remove from heat and allow the apples to remain in the syrup overnight. Next morning, pack the apples into sterilized jars and fill with syrup to within ½-inch from the tops. Complete seals and process for 20 minutes in a boiling-water bath.

Pickled Cucumber Chips

Yield: 8 pints

4 qts. medium-sized cucumbers, sliced
1½ cups onions, sliced
2 large cloves garlic
⅓ cup salt
2 qts. ice cubes
2 cups honey
1½ teaspoons turmeric
1½ teaspoons celery seed
2 tablespoons mustard seed
3 cups vinegar

Wash cucumbers, scrubbing lightly with a vegetable brush. Drain well. Slice into ¼-inch slices; discard ends. Add sliced onion and garlic to the cucumbers in a large bowl or crock, add salt and mix thoroughly. Cover with ice and let stand for 3 hours. Drain, removing garlic cloves. Combine spices and vinegar and heat just to a boil. Add honey, cucumbers, and onion slices and heat for 5 minutes. Pack hot into hot sterilized jars to ½-inch from tops. Complete seals and process for 5 minutes in a boiling-water bath.

Pickled Eggs

15-18 eggs

Carefully shell hard-boiled eggs and pack them into hot sterilized jars. Cover with the following boiling liquid.

3 cups vinegar
1 cup water
1 teaspoon salt
1 tablespoon pickling spices

Seal immediately. Store in the refrigerator.

O-Shinko [Japanese Pickled Greens]

20 lbs. greens of turnips, lettuce, collards, beets, dandelions, chard, or Chinese cabbage
1½ cups salt

Shred the greens. Sprinkle a little salt on the bottom of a large crock. Place a layer of greens over the salt and sprinkle lightly with more salt. Continue layering this way. Add enough water to fill half the crock. Place a plate on top of the greens and weigh down with a heavy object (something that weighs at least 20 lbs.). Store in a cool place. After several days, the plate will be entirely submerged in liquid and the pickle is ready to eat. It's good served with tamari sauce.

Pickled Mushrooms

Yield: 4 half-pints

6 cups small mushrooms
½ cup lemon juice
4 cups water
2 cups vinegar
1 teaspoon salt
1 teaspoon oregano
3 bay leaves
1 teaspoon sweet basil
2 cloves garlic
1½ cups olive oil

Combine the lemon juice with the water in a large saucepan. Add the clean mushrooms and bring to a boil. Simmer for 5 minutes. Drain the mushrooms and place them in the vinegar. Cover and let stand overnight. Drain. Mix the spices with the olive oil. Pack the mushrooms into clean sterilized jars. Pour the oil to within ½-inch from tops. Complete seals and process for 20 minutes in a boiling-water bath.

Pickled Okra

Yield: 6 pints

12 cups small okra
1 quart vinegar
2 cups water
½ cup salt
garlic, 1 clove per pint
onion rings, 2 rings per pint
dried red pepper, ½ tsp. per pint
dill seed, 1 tsp. per pint

Cut the stem end off the okra without cutting into the pod part. Place in a large bowl and cover with ice water. Soak for 1 hour. Drain and pack okra into hot sterilized jars along with the garlic, onion, red pepper and dill seed. Heat the vinegar, water and salt to a boil and pour over the okra to within ½-inch of the tops of the jars. Complete seals. Cool the jars and check for a complete seal. Turn jars upside down and store. They are ready to eat in about 2 weeks.

This recipe comes from a true southern belle who makes delicious pickled okra!

Pickled Onions

Yield: 4 pints

3 qts. small white onions
½ cup salt
4 cups water
1 chili pepper
½ teaspoon peppercorns
4 inches of ginger root
¼ cup honey
6 cups vinegar

Scald and peel the onions. Dissolve salt in 4 cups of water in a glass bowl or crock. Add the onions and enough water to cover. Let stand overnight; rinse well and drain. Steam the onions for 1 minute. Spoon into hot sterilized jars along with bits of finely cut chili pepper, peppercorns, and finely sliced ginger root. Heat the honey and vinegar together just to a boil. Pour over the onions to within ½-inch from tops of jars. Complete seals and process for 15 minutes in a boiling-water bath.

These onions are delicious with curried foods.

Pickled Peppers

Yield: 8 pints

Any variety of peppers may be used.

4 quarts peppers
1½ cups salt
3 cloves garlic
2 tablespoons prepared horseradish
10 cups vinegar
2 cups water

If the peppers are really large, cut them into strips. Otherwise, cut two small slits in each pepper. Dissolve salt in about 4 quarts water, and pour over the peppers. Let stand for 16 hours. Drain, rinse well, and drain again. Combine the garlic, horseradish, vinegar, and water and simmer for 15 minutes. Remove garlic. Pack the peppers into hot sterilized jars to within ¼-inch from tops. Pour enough liquid over the peppers to just cover them. Complete seals and process for 10 minutes in a boiling-water bath.

Pickled Petals

Flowers and buds of:
roses
violets
nasturtiums
chrysanthemums
calendula or
primrose
honey
distilled white vinegar
mace or mint sprigs

Carefully remove sepals from the base of the flower, and the stems and stamens from the inside. Layer the flowers in a jar, covering each layer with a drizzle of honey. When the jar is full, pour boiling vinegar to within ½-inch of the top. Add a sprig of mace or mint. Complete the seals. Pickled petals are ready to mix with salads or to garnish a relish tray in about 4-5 days. They also make attractive, colorful jars to give as gifts or to adorn a kitchen shelf.

Sunchoke Pickles

Yield: 4 pints

8 cups peeled and cubed sunchokes
1 cup salt
1 gallon water
¾ cup honey
1 clove garlic
1½ teaspoons turmeric
2 tablespoons pickling spices
1 qt. apple cider vinegar

Make a brine using the salt and water. Stir until the salt dissolves. Put the sunchokes into the brine and let stand overnight. Rinse, drain, and pack into clean jars. Combine remaining ingredients and let simmer for 20 minutes. Pour over the sunchokes to within 1 inch from tops of jars. Complete seals and process for 10 minutes in a boiling-water bath.

Sunchokes are also known as Jerusalem Artichokes

Sweet Gherkins

Yield: 10 pints

30 small gherkins
2 cups lime
2 gallons water
2 qts. vinegar
4 cups honey
2 teaspoons whole cloves
1 teaspoon salt

Dissolve the lime in water. Pour over the gherkins to cover. Let stand for 24 hours and rinse well, then let stand for 3 hours in clear water. Drain. Mix the vinegar, honey, cloves, and salt and heat just enough to dissolve the honey. Pour the mixture over the drained cucumbers and let them stand overnight. Next morning, bring to a boil and cook for 30-35 minutes. Pack the gherkins into hot sterilized jars to within ½-inch from tops. Pour in the brine to just cover them. Complete seals; process for 5 minutes in a boiling-water bath.

Zucchini Bread-and-Butter Pickles

Yield: 6 qts.

2 qts. apple cider vinegar
2 cups honey
6 tablespoons salt
4 teaspoons celery seed
4 teaspoons dill seed
2 teaspoons ground mustard
8 qts. fresh zucchini, sliced
2 qts. onion, sliced

Bring vinegar, honey, and spices to a boil. Pour over the zucchini and onions. Let stand for 2 hours. Heat mixture to a boil and cook for 3 minutes. They will get mushy if cooked longer. Pack into hot sterilized jars. Insert a knife down the edge of the jars to remove any air bubbles. Complete seals; process for 15 minutes in a boiling-water bath.

Season's End Mixed Pickles

Yield: 8 pints

2 cups sliced cucumbers
2 cups chopped cauliflower
2 cups sweet peppers
2 cups chopped carrots
2 cups sliced onions
2 cups chopped green tomatoes
2 cups string beans, cut into 1-inch pieces
2 cups chopped celery
2 tablespoons celery seed
4 tablespoons mustard seed
4 cups vinegar
2 cups honey
4 tablespoons turmeric

Soak the cucumbers, peppers, cabbage, tomatoes, and onions overnight in a solution of 1 cup salt to 4 qts. water. Drain well. Cook the carrots and beans in boiling water until tender and drain. Mix all the vegetables together with the remaining ingredients and boil for 8 minutes. Pack into hot sterilized jars to within ½-inch from tops. Complete seals; process for 5 minutes in a boiling-water bath.

Sweet Mixed Pickles

Yield: 6 pints

2 qts. cubed cucumbers
2 qts. tiny pickling onions, peeled
1 large head cauliflower,
  broken into flowerets
2 large sweet red peppers,
  seeded and chopped
8 cups vinegar
2½ cups honey
1 cup salt
½ teaspoon turmeric
2 tablespoons mixed pickling spices
4 inches of stick cinnamon
12 whole cloves
2 teaspoons mustard seed

Combine the vegetables, sprinkle with salt, cover with cold water, and let stand overnight. Drain, rinse in fresh water and drain again. Combine the vinegar, honey, and turmeric in a large kettle. Tie the spices in a square of cheesecloth and add them to the vinegar mixture. Place over medium heat and bring to a boil. Cook for 10 minutes. Add well-drained vegetables, bring to a boil. Cook for 5 minutes. Pack into hot sterilized jars to within ½-inch from tops. Complete seals; process for 10 minutes in a boiling-water bath.

Ginger Pears

Yield· 4.pints

12 large pears, firmly ripe
4 cups honey
juice of 4 lemons
grated rind of 2 lemons
2 ounces ginger root
4 cups water

Wash, peel, and core the pears and cut them into small pieces. Mix remaining ingredients together and slowly bring to a boil. Add the pears; boil slowly until pears are just tender and syrup is thickish. Pack into hot sterilized jars to within ½-inch from top. Complete seals. Process for 10 minutes in a boiling-water bath.

Peach Mangoes

Yield: 6 pints

4 qts. peaches
chopped tomato
grated horseradish
mustard seed
3 cups honey
1 qt. vinegar

Use only sound, ripe, freestone peaches. Skin the peaches, cut them in half, and remove the pits. Fill the cavities with the finely cut tomato, grated horseradish, and mustard seed. Match halves and tie each one together with a piece of strong thread. Pack into hot sterilized jars. Mix together the honey and vinegar and heat to a boil. Pour over the peaches to within ½-inch from top. Complete seals. Process in a boiling-water bath for 10 minutes.

Pickled Peaches, Pears or Apricots

Yield: 6 quarts

12 lbs. peaches, pears, or apricots
  (about 6 qts.)
1 qt. vinegar
6 cups honey
1 tablespoon ground cloves
1 small piece ginger root
5 sticks cinnamon

Peel the peaches or pears; apricots may be used unpeeled. If they are to remain exposed to the air for any length of time, soak in a mixture of 2 tablespoons salt and 2 tablespoons vinegar to 1 gallon of water. Do not leave fruit in the mixture for longer than 20 minutes, and rinse well before packing. Make a syrup of the vinegar and honey. Tie the cloves and the ginger root in a square of cheesecloth; add to the syrup. The cinnamon sticks can be placed directly in the syrup. Heat to a boil. Add the fruit and cook until it is tender. Remove from heat, cover, and let stand overnight. Next morning, remove the spices and pack into sterilized jars. Fill with syrup to within ½-inch from the tops of jars. Complete seals. Process for 20 minutes in a boiling-water bath.

Spiced Plums

Yield: 7 pints

4 qts. plums
2 cups vinegar
3 cups honey
1 tablespoon cloves
1 tablespoon cinnamon
1 teaspoon allspice

Wash and dry the plums. Put them in a large porcelain bowl that is heat-proof. Combine the honey, vinegar, and spices. Bring to a boil and cook for 10 minutes. Pour over the plums. Cover and let stand overnight. Drain the liquid and bring to a boil. Add the plums and cook until plums are clear but not broken. Pack into hot sterilized jars. Cover plums with the syrup to within ½-inch from tops. Complete seals. Process for 10 minutes in a boiling-water bath.

Watermelon Rind Pickles

Yield: 8 pints

Rind of 1 watermelon
hot water
3 cups honey
1¼ cups cider vinegar
2 teaspoons fresh grated lemon peel
½ cup fresh squeezed lemon juice
1 teaspoon cinnamon
½ teaspoon cloves

Peel skins and most of the pink flesh from the rind. Cut into I-inch cubes. Place in a large kettle, cover with hot water, and bring to a boil. Cook until rind is tender but not soft—about 25 minutes. Drain. Place in a large glass bowl or earthenware crock. Combine remaining ingredients in a sauce pan and bring to a boil. Pour over the melon rind. Let stand overnight. Next morning, pour off the syrup, bring it to a boil, and pour it back over rind. Let stand overnight again. The third day, bring both rind and syrup to a boil. Pack rind in hot sterilized jars, covering with the syrup to within ½-inch from tops. Complete seals. Process for 5 minutes in a boiling-water bath.

Beet Relish

Yield: 3-4 pints

1 qt. chopped, cooked beets
1 small head chopped cabbage
1 cup chopped onions
2 cups chopped sweet red peppers
1 tablespoon salt
1 tablespoon prepared horseradish
¾ cup honey
3 cups apple cider vinegar

Combine all ingredients. Simmer for 10 minutes, then bring to a boil. Pack into hot sterilized jars to within ⅛-inch from tops. Process for 15 minutes in a boiling-water bath.

Chow Chow

Yield: 6 pints

12 lbs. green tomatoes
8 large onions
11 green bell peppers
6 red sweet peppers
3 tablespoons salt
1 qt. vinegar
¾ cup honey
2 teaspoons dry mustard
1 teaspoon turmeric
½ teaspoon ground ginger
2 teaspoons celery seed
1 teaspoon mustard seed

Chop all vegetables uniformly. Combine them and sprinkle with salt. Let stand for 6 hours in a cool place. Drain well. Combine vinegar, honey, and spices; simmer for 10 minutes. Add the vegetables; simmer for 10 minutes more. Bring to a boil and pack into hot sterilized jars to within ⅛-inch from top. Process for 10 minutes in a boiling-water bath.

Corn Relish

Yield: 8 pints

18 ears corn (2 qts. kernels)
2 cups chopped sweet red pepper
2 cups chopped green pepper
4 cups chopped celery
1 cup chopped onion
½ cup honey
1 qt. vinegar
2 tablespoons salt
2 teaspoons celery seed
2 tablespoons hot mustard
1 teaspoon turmeric
¼ cup unbleached white flour

Cook the corn on the cob for about 3 minutes. Dip into cold water and drain. Cut the kernels from the cob. Combine all the vegetables except the corn with the honey, vinegar, salt, and celery seed. Simmer 15 minutes. Mix the mustard, turmeric, and flour with ½ cup water. Add it along with the corn to the other ingredients. Simmer for 5 minutes, stirring constantly. Pack into hot sterilized jars to within ¼-inch from top. Complete seals. Process for 10 minutes in a boiling-water bath.

Cucumber Relish

Yield: 6 pints

4 cups cucumbers
1 cup green pepper
½ cup sweet red pepper
3 cups onion
3 cups celery
¼ cup salt
1¾ cups honey
2 cups vinegar
1 tablespoon celery seed
1 tablespoon mustard seed
1 tablespoon coriander

Finely chop all the vegetables. Combine in a large bowl. Sprinkle with salt, cover with cold water, and let stand 5 hours. Drain thoroughly in a colander, pressing out excess liquid. Combine honey, vinegar, and spices. Bring to a boil. Stir in drained vegetables and simmer for 10 minutes. Pack into hot sterilized jars to within ½-inch from top. Complete seals. Process for 10 minutes in a boiling-water bath.

Curry Relish

Yield: 8 pints

16 medium-size green tomatoes
6 large red tomatoes
1 small head cabbage
3 medium-size onions
3 stalks celery
2 medium-size green peppers
2 sweet red peppers
1 cup chopped cucumbers
½ cup salt
2 qts. vinegar
2 cups honey
1 tablespoon celery seed
1 tablespoon mustard seed
1 tablespoon ground cinnamon
1 teaspoon ground ginger
½ teaspoon ground cloves
2 teaspoons curry powder
2 cups raisins

Chop all the vegetables to a uniform size. Mix together, sprinkle with the salt, and mix thoroughly. Let stand for 16 hours in a cool place. Drain thoroughly. Combine the honey, vinegar, spices, and garlic; simmer 10 minutes. Add the vegetables and the raisins; simmer for 30 minutes. Bring to a boil and pack into hot sterilized jars to within ⅛-inch from top. Complete seals. Process for 15 minutes in a boiling-water bath.

Horseradish

Yield: 2 half-pints

1 cup grated fresh horseradish root
½ cup white vinegar
¼ teaspoon salt

Wash the horseradish roots, scrubbing with a vegetable brush. Remove the outer skin, then grate. Combine with the vinegar and salt. Pack into clean jars and seal. Keep refrigerated.

Hot Salsa

Yield: 6 pints

5 lbs. ripe tomatoes
2 lbs. hot chilies (long green)
1 lb. onions
2 teaspoons salt
½ teaspoon black pepper
⅓ cup lemon juice

Chop the onions and chilies into small pieces. Peel the tomatoes and chop into small pieces. Combine all ingredients and bring to a boil. Pack into hot sterilized jars to within ¼-inch from top. Process for 5 minutes in a boiling-water bath.

Piccalilli

Yield: 5 pints

6 lbs. green tomatoes
1 large green pepper
1 hot red pepper
1 onion
1 cup salt
6 cups vinegar
½ cup honey
½ teaspoon ground ginger
½ teaspoon ground cinnamon
½ teaspoon ground allspice
1 tablespoon mustard seed
½ cup freshly grated horseradish

Chop the tomatoes, peppers, and onion. Sprinkle with salt, cover with water, and let soak overnight. Combine the vinegar, honey, ginger, cinnamon, and mustard. Drain the tomato mixture and simmer in the vinegar for 3 minutes. Do not boil. Add the horseradish. Pack into hot sterilized jars to within ¼-inch from top. Complete seals. Process for 10 minutes in a boiling-water bath.

Sunchoke Relish

Yield: 2 pints

2½ cups peeled, sliced sunchokes
1½ cups chopped green pepper
½ cup pimientos
½ cup chopped onions
1 cup vinegar
2½ teaspoons salt
4 tablespoons honey

Put the sunchokes in a solution of 2 tablespoons lemon juice to 1 qt. water as they are sliced. Chop the peppers, pimientos, and onions. Drain the sunchokes. Combine all ingredients in a pan and heat to a boil. Simmer for 5 minutes, stirring frequently. Spoon into hot sterilized jars to within ¼-inch from top. Complete seals. Process for 10 minutes in a boiling-water bath.

Sunchokes are also known as Jerusalem Artichokes.

Uncooked Relish

Yield: 5 pints

2 cups sweet red peppers
2 cups green peppers
2 cups onions
1 cabbage
½ cup celery
5 tablespoons salt
2 teaspoons celery seed
1 teaspoon coriander
1 teaspoon cumin
1 cup honey
1 qt. vinegar

Chop all the vegetables uniformly and drain their liquid. Mix vegetables with salt and let stand overnight. In the morning, drain all excess liquid. Add the spices, honey, and vinegar to the vegetables and mix well. Pack into sterilized jars to within ½-inch from the tops. Complete seals. Process for 15 minutes in a boiling-water bath.

Zucchini Relish

Yield: 5 pints

4 cups chopped zucchini
3 cups chopped carrots
4½ cups chopped onion
1½ cups chopped pepper
⅓ cup salt
¼ cup salt
2¼ cups vinegar
⅓ cup honey
1 teaspoon celery seed
¾ teaspoon powdered mustard
1 teaspoon turmeric
1 teaspoon curry powder

Combine chopped vegetables and sprinkle with salt. Let stand overnight in the refrigerator. Drain and rinse with cold water. Mix together the remaining ingredients. Add the zucchini mixture. Simmer for 20 minutes until the vegetables are just tender, but still crisp. Pack into hot sterilized jars to within ½-inch from tops. Complete seals. Process for 20 minutes in a boiling-water bath.

Apple Chutney

Yield: 6 pints

12 apples (pippins are best)
6 green tomatoes
4 white onions, small
3 green peppers
1 cup raisins
2 tablespoons mustard seed
2 cups honey
4 cups vinegar
2 teaspoons salt
2 tablespoons ground ginger
2 teaspoons ground allspice
1 clove garlic, crushed

Cube the apples. Chop the tomatoes, onions, and peppers. Mix together with the remaining ingredients and simmer it all until thick. Stir often as it begins to thicken. Spoon into hot sterilized jars to within ¼-inch from tops. Complete seals. Process for 10 minutes in a boiling-water bath.

Fragrant-Tree-Island Chutney

Yield: 3 pints

2½ cups crushed pineapple
1 mango, chopped
2 cups golden raisins
½ cup honey
1 teaspoon salt
¼ teaspoon ground ginger
1 teaspoon ground allspice
½ teaspoon ground cinnamon
⅛ teaspoon ground cloves
¼ teaspoon cayenne

Combine all ingredients and cook over moderate heat to a boil. Reduce heat and simmer the mixture for 45 minutes or until thick. Spoon into hot sterilized jars to within ¼-inch from tops. Complete seals. Process for 20 minutes in a boiling-water bath.

Hot-But-Sweet Chutney

Yield: 4 half-pints

1 orange
3 apples
2 peaches, mangos or nectarines
1 lemon
1 onion
1 cup honey
1 cup vinegar
1 cup water
2 tablespoons fresh ginger root, finely chopped
2 small hot chilies
¾ cup raisins
1 teaspoon peppercorns
1 teaspoon allspice
1 teaspoon mustard seed
1 teaspoon whole cloves
1 teaspoon celery seed

Chop the fruits and onion into small pieces. Combine with honey, vinegar, and water. Tie the spices in a square of cheesecloth. Cook it all for about 20 minutes, then add the raisins and continue to cook until thick. Remove spice bag. Spoon into hot sterilized jars to within ¼-inch from tops. Complete seals. Process for 20 minutes in a boiling-water bath.

Plum Chutney

Yield: 4 half-pints

1 lb. Damson Plums
1½ cups dark honey
½ cup apple cider vinegar
1¼ cups raisins
10 prunes, cooked and pitted
1 apple, diced
¼ teaspoon cayenne
½ teaspoon ground allspice
½ teaspoon ground cloves
½ teaspoon black pepper
½ teaspoon ground cardamom
½ teaspoon ground cinnamon

Cook plums in just enough water to cover them. When soft, remove the pits. Combine with remaining ingredients and simmer for about 30 minutes. Spoon into hot sterilized jars to within ¼-inch of the tops. Complete seals. Process for 20 minutes in a boiling-water bath.

Tomato Chutney

Yield: 6 pints

16 large ripe tomatoes
3 large apples
3 large pears
3 large peaches
2 onions, chopped
1 cup apple cider vinegar
1½ cups honey
1 tablespoon salt
½ cup mixed pickling spices

Plunge tomatoes, apples, pears, and peaches into boiling water, then immerse in cold water. Core and peel, then chop fine. Mix all the ingredients together and boil until thick. Spoon hot mixture into hot sterilized jars to within ½-inch of the tops. Complete seals. Process in a boiling-water bath for 5 minutes.

Tomato Catsup

Yield: 4 pints

½ cup chopped celery
1 cup chopped onions
18 lbs. tomatoes, washed and stemmed
3 tablespoons salt
⅓ cup honey
1 tablespoon paprika
¼ teaspoon cayenne pepper
1 tablespoon powdered mustard
2 cups vinegar
1 tablespoon whole peppercorns
1 tablespoon whole allspice
1 tablespoon mustard seed
4 bay leaves
4 small hot chilies
1 tablespoon dried basil

Cook the tomatoes, celery, and onions until soft. It is not necessary to add any water because the tomatoes provide enough juice. When soft, press the pulp through a sieve to measure about 7 quarts of puree. Put the tomato puree in a large pot. Add the salt, honey, paprika, and cayenne. Blend the powdered mustard with a bit of tomato liquid to prevent lumping and add it to the mixture. Tie all the spices in a cheesecloth bag and add to the mixture. Simmer until thick—about 1½ hours. Add the vinegar during the last 15 minutes of cooking. Remove the spices. Spoon hot into hot sterilized jars to within ¼-inch of the tops. Complete seals. Process for 10 minutes in a boiling-water bath.

Chapter 5

Dried Foods

Dried Foods

Drying foods is the oldest and most practical method of preserving foods. The essence of the flavor remains, only the water is removed. Dried foods make a tasteful addition to a pantry of canned goods. There are no hard and fast techniques for this natural method of preserving. Considerable variety exists in the recommendations for treatment of foods before drying and in drying times and temperatures. Fruits may be honey-dipped before drying or simply sliced and dried. Some vegetables require blanching beforehand, others need only to be chopped or sliced into small pieces. Drying may be done outdoors in the sun, indoors by the stove, or in a drying oven. When drying is completed the product requires little storage space since its bulk is only about 1/10th of its original size.

What Happens When You Dry It

Bacteria, molds, and yeasts cannot survive without sufficient water. The drying process removes enough water from the plant cells to prevent their hosting the growth of spoilage organisms during storage. The food's natural acidity (pH-factor) determines the amount of moisture that may remain in the dried product. More water may be left in high-acid foods (such as fruits), since they are more resistant to spoilage micro-organisms than are low-acid foods (such as vegetables). Dried foods generally contain about 10 to 20 percent of their original moisture. Foods containing less are classified "dehydrated" or "evaporated".

The faster the drying process, the more vitamins and minerals are retained in the dried product. Contents of vitamins A and C are lower in the dried product than in the fresh food due to the natural oxidation process that occurs when any food is exposed to air. The honey-lemon dip recommended for fruits prior to drying greatly aids the preservation of vitamins by slowing down the oxidation process. Since dried foods weigh less than they did in fresh form, the pound-for-pound vitamin and mineral content is higher in dried products.

Selection and Preparation of Foods to Dry

Fruits and vegetables should be selected for drying when they are fully ripe and the natural sugar content is at its peak. Blemished or bruised produce should not be used; it does not keep well and may cause a whole tray to mold while drying.

Fruits may be dried in pieces or as a puree. A puree is poured onto waxed paper to dry. The finished product is a fruit leather which is easily stored in rolls and is peeled from the paper to eat.

Foods to be dried should be washed, trimmed, and sliced or chopped. Produce left in large pieces (such as apricot or peach halves) should be placed in a single, even layer on the drying surface. Foods to be dried in smaller pieces (such as peas or corn or finely chopped produce) should be spread about one-inch deep on the drying trays. Turn food once or twice daily to insure even drying and to prevent the formation of clumps. You can turn larger pieces individually; smaller pieces may be stirred with the hands or with a spatula.

Dried vegetables are also a valuable food source. Although beans and peas are the most commonly dried vegetables, produce such as broccoli and tomatoes make an excellent vegetable seasoning powder when dried and finely ground. Dried vegetables also make a great quick soup stock. Except for onions, vegetables should be blanched in steam or in boiling water before they are dried. This sets the color, checks the ripening process and also hastens the drying time by softening the tissues. Blanching by steam is preferable because boiling dissolves the nutrients in the water. Vegetables which are blanched before drying require less soaking time if they are to be reconstituted later.

Dried herbs are an excellent addition to the pantry. Gather them just before they flower and hang them in bundles upside down in the shade to dry. Smaller bundles dry faster. A spot in a warm kitchen or attic which is out of direct sunlight is an excellent place to dry herbs.

To Prevent Darkening and Hardening

Dried fruit is more appealing when it has a bright, natural color and a soft texture. Most commercial drying operations and many home dryers sulphur the fruit before drying it to retain its natural color, to help prevent molding, and to repel insects. Since sulphur dioxide has been shown to be harmful to the body and to destroy fine fruit flavors, I do not recommend its use. There are several quick dips, recipes for which are given on page 181, that serve as alternatives to sulphuring. They help retain good color, preserve the fruit and slow the oxidation process. The dipping occurs just after the food has been chopped and before the pieces are spread on the drying trays.

Blanching and Checking

Blanching is a simple process and can be done by steaming or boiling. Foods are first plunged into boiling water or into steam to stop the enzyme action, then into cold water to stop further cooking. Steam blanching saves more nutritive value and flavor than does water blanching.

A pressure cooker or a large pot with a lid makes a good steamer. Put two or three inches of water in the pot and heat to boiling. Set a wire basket, steamer rack or colander in the pot. Prepare the vegetables by slicing or cubing. Layer them about 2½ inches deep in the basket or rack of the steamer pot. Cover tightly and heat until each piece is hot, about 3 to 5 minutes. Exact blanching times are listed with each recipe. Be sure the vegetables are packed loosely, to allow even circulation of steam.

To blanch by boiling, any large pot may be used It's best to use a large amount of boiling water and a small amount of food so the temperature of the water is not greatly reduced when the vegetables are added. Lower the vegetables into the boiling water in a wire basket and blanch for the time indicated in the recipe.

Fruits, including peppers and tomatos, do not require blanching. Vegetables, such as peas, spinach, chard, and juicy sweet corn, should always be blanched. Corn and beans which have been allowed to dry partially before harvesting should not be blanched before spreading on trays to complete the drying process.

Checking the skins helps remove the natural wax coating from such fruits as cherries, figs, grapes, and certain berries. Checking also allows the internal moisture to be drawn through to the surface and then to evaporate. This method is similar to blanching, but quicker. The fruit is given a very quick dip into briskly boiling water and is then dunked into very cold water. The fruit should then be drained thoroughly and spread in a single layer on an absorbent towel to remove surface moisture.

How to Tell When it's Dry

Fruit is dried when it feels dry and leathery on the outside but slightly moist on the inside. Most fruits will take at least six hours to dry. Different drying times depend on the size of the pieces and the particular drying conditions. When it is hot, fruit contains more moisture, so remove a few pieces from the tray to cool before you test for dryness. Cut a few pieces in half; if the center has a darker, wet color, it needs to dry longer. Apples, peaches, and apricots should be pliable and leathery.

Vegetables should be allowed to dry until they feel brittle. Most vegetables take from four to twelve hours to dry and are not harmed if allowed to dry longer. Peas should be shriveled and wrinkled, corn dimpled and slightly transparent, and beans firm and smooth.

Storage

Store dried foods in air-tight containers such as glass jars or metal cans with tight-fitting tops. Check the food after three or four days to make sure that any moisture from the less dried pieces has been evenly distributed. If the food seems to be too moist, causing small beads of moisture or fogging on the inside of the jar, return it to the drying trays or food dryer. Dried foods should be stored in a cool, dry place where they will keep for several years.

Techniques for Drying Foods

Heat and air are the two necessary elements in food drying; insects and damp weather are the two "elements" to avoid. You can meet all these requirements whether drying directly in sunlight or using artificial heat.

Sunshine is the most practical heat source for drying. A large quantity of food may be rapidly dried at one time simply by exposing it to the sun's healthful rays. When the weather is damp, overcast or rainy, however, drying must be done indoors in an oven, on top of the furnace, or in a specially constructed food dryer.

Drying Trays

Anything that has a flat surface can serve as a drying tray, although a ventilated bottom is best because it increases air circulation. Drying trays can be constructed by making a wooden frame, then stretching wire diagonally from corner to corner for support. Several layers of cheesecloth are stretched over the frame to form the "tray". Cheesecloth is generally available in a width of 36", so be sure to construct your frames to fit.

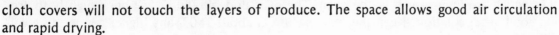

Place the food on the cheesecloth and cover it with another cloth-covered frame. The cover tray will keep insects from landing on the food. With 2x2-inch boards construct the frames so the cheese-cloth covers will not touch the layers of produce. The space allows good air circulation and rapid drying.

Window screens with wooden frames also make excellent drying trays. Cover them with two layers of cheesecloth or an old sheet, since the fruit may become toxic from contact with certain metals.

Another idea for wooden trays is to nail ½-inch wood strips to the bottom of a wood frame. Place them about ½-inch apart so the food won't slip through. Wooden dowels also work well when nailed inside a frame. Remember to make your frame sides high enough (2 inches) to stack another on top and allow good air flow. These trays can then be covered with a layer of cheesecloth.

Sun Drying

During the sunny hot season, foods can easily be dried out-of-doors. Trays should be placed at least a foot off the ground to allow for good air flow. Placing the supports (table legs or bricks) in pans of water protects the produce against crawling insects such as ants. The food should be turned once or twice a day to insure even drying. At night the trays should be covered with a sheet of glass or plastic, or brought indoors to prevent dew from settling on the foods, since it may otherwise re-absorb the moisture it lost during the day.

To intensify the heat of the sun and hasten the drying process, a simple solar dryer can be constructed. A piece of glass tilted toward the sun at an angle of 35° will magnify the heat and lower the relative humidity inside the covered area. The open area between glass and tray should be covered with screen or cheesecloth to keep out flying insects.

Oven Drying

In climates where summer rains are frequent, the kitchen stove can easily become a good food dryer. If the drying trays are the right size they can be placed directly into the oven. You can also place foods on the oven racks or, if the slats are too far apart, on cooling racks which are then placed in the oven. The oven door should be left open slightly to provide good air circulation. Keep the temperature at about 150°; any higher temperature will cook the food. It takes only three or four hours to dry the produce. Turning every hour or so will ensure even drying.

If you have a wood-burner, suspend the racks above it to dry the produce. Dry wood-heat is excellent for drying foods.

Food Dryers

Special food dryers can be constructed for those who wish to do a lot of drying but do not find sun-drying feasible. The United States Department of Agriculture, Farmers Bulletin No. 984, gives directions for making several types and sizes of dryers. Material is also available from government Agriculture Extension Services in many states.

Helpful Hints

1. Have your equipment ready before you pick fruit for drying.

2. If you use metal trays or screens, cover them with cloth. It's best to use wooden, slatted trays or cloth-covered screens.

3. Always provide good air circulation.

4. Wooden produce crates sawed horizontally in several sections make excellent drying trays.

5. When drying foods outdoors, cover the tray with a screen, another cheesecloth-covered tray, or simply a layer of cheesecloth thumbtacked down.

6. Always bring the produce indoors at night or cover it up so moisture does not re-settle on the food.

Equipment

Drying trays or racks
Cheesecloth
Table top or low roof
Shallow pans of water to deter
   crawling insects.

Honey Lemon Dip

½ cup honey
juice of one lemon
½ cup water

Slightly heat the mixture so the honey fully dissolves. Dip the prepared fruit into the mixture, then spread on the drying trays. The honey acts as a natural preservative, while the lemon helps to retain the fruit color.

Vitamin C Dip

2½ teaspoons ascorbic acid (Vitamin C)
1 cup water

Dissolve the ascorbic acid in the water. Dip the prepared fruit into the mixture, then spread onto the drying trays. This method acts as a good antioxidant and will treat about 5 quarts of cut fruit. Ascorbic acid is available in most natural food or health food stores.

Salt-water Dip

4 tablespoons salt
1 gallon water

Soak fruit in above solution for 5 minutes, then spread onto the drying trays. This dip helps to retain good color in the dried product.

Apples

Choose firm, mature late autumn or early winter varieties. Winesap, Greening, Red Delicious, and Golden Delicious are excellent varieties. Peel, trim, and core the apples and cut them into ¼- to ⅛-inch rings. It is best to prepare one tray at a time, putting each filled tray in the hot sun immediately.

Turn fruit occasionally during the day and cover the tray or bring it in at night. When dry, apples should be rubbery and chewy, not hard and crisp. No moisture should be present when cut or squeezed. Store in an air-tight container in a cool, dry place.

I have found that the ascorbic acid dip works best for treating apples for darkening. They may also be dunked in a weak saline solution.

To stove-top or oven dry, prepare as above, spread on a wire rack, and dry at 120 to 150 degrees Fahrenheit.

Apricots

Pick the apricots when they are just ripe enough to drop from the tree, don't wait until they fall. Wash, cut in half, and remove the pits. Treat them for darkening with the honey-lemon mixture or the ascorbic acid dip. Spread them cut side up on the tray and place them in the sun. Cover or bring in each night. When dry, apricots will have a leathery look and feel, with no moisture present when cut. Store in an air-tight container in a cool, dry place.

To stove-top or oven dry, prepare as above, spread cut side down on a wire rack, and dry at 120 to 150 degrees.

Bananas

Allow the bananas to ripen until the skins have a brown, flecked appearance. Peel and slice very thinly. Spread on cheesecloth tray to dry in the hot sun. When dry, bananas will be crisp. Store slices in tightly covered jars.

Beans

The easiest way to dry beans is in the garden, if you live in an area that doesn't get early rains. Allow the pods to stay on the vines until the vines are dry and shriveled. Pull the vines and pluck off the pods. If the weather is damp, pull the vines and hang upside down in a dry place until the pods are well-shriveled. Shell the beans and store in jars.

If the rains come early, pick the pods from the vines when they turn yellow. Spread the pods on drying racks and dry until they are well-shriveled. Shell the beans and store in jars.

Bean pods can also be strung and hung in the attic until ready to use. Simply harvest the pods when they are yellowish and string with a large needle and heavy thread.

To stove-top or oven dry, pull the pods when they begin to yellow. Shell immediately to avoid mildew. Spread on trays and dry at 150 degrees.

Beets

Boil young tender beets for 20 minutes, then slip off the skins and remove the root end. Chop into small cubes. Allow to cool, then spread on drying trays. Dry beets are very firm. To stove-top or oven dry, prepare as above, spread on trays and dry at a low heat until brittle.

Dried beets, along with other dried vegetables and herbs, can make an excellent soup stock. Grind the dried vegetables into a fine powder and mix with desired herbs. Store in a tightly sealed jar until ready to use.

Candied Dried Fruits

Candied fruits usually consist of cherries, pineapple, orange, citron, lemon, and grapefruit. They can be done separately or mixed together. Wash and pit or peel; remove any white membrane from the citrus fruits. Cook in a medium to heavy syrup (*see* p. 93) for two hours until the fruit is translucent. Drain and place on drying racks. Dry in the sun. When thoroughly dry, pack in waxed paper-lined tins or jars. Layers may be dribbled with honey if desired.

Carrots

Scrub carrots and slice off ends. Cut into thin slices and steam blanch until tender, 6 to 7 minutes. Spread on trays and dry in the sun until very crisp and brittle. To stove-top or oven dry, prepare as above. Spread on drying trays over a low heat.

Dried carrots are good in soups and also make an excellent vegetable broth or vegetable powder when combined with other dried vegetables and herbs. Store in sealed jars.

Sweet Corn

Dried sweet corn makes a delicious cooked vegetable. The corn must be gathered in the milk stage and processed immediately. Husk the corn and plunge into rapidly boiling water for 5 minutes; this sets the milk in the kernels. Then plunge into ice cold water to stop the cooking. When cool enough to handle, cut from the cob, being careful not to cut into the cob. Spread on trays ¼-inch deep and stir several times while drying. Drying in hot sun takes 1 to 2 days. To stove-top or oven dry, prepare as above but spread trays 1½-inches deep. Dry with a low heat for about two days. Stir several times to dry evenly throughout. When dry, the corn is brittle and a piece cracks clean when broken. Store in jars or tins.

One good way to prepare sweet corn is:

1 cup dried corn   *2 cups water*

Soak for 2 hours; do not drain. Add:

½ tsp. salt   *1 Tbs. honey*   *pepper*

Cover and cook slowly until tender. Add butter. For creamed corn, add 2 Tbs. milk before serving.

Popcorn or Flint Corn

The corn should be allowed to mature on the stalk and become partly dry before it is harvested. When harvested, peel the husks back from the partly dried ears and braid or tie them together. Hang in the sun to finish the drying process. The hard kernels will rub easily from the cob when they are dry and should remain plump.

Flint corn is usually ground into cornmeal.

Currants

The longer currants remain on the bush, the sweeter they become. When ready, spread thinly on drying trays and dry in the sun. For stove-top or oven drying, spread thinly and dry over a low heat. Store dried currants in an air-tight container.

Figs

Use small figs or ones that have partly dried on the tree. Check the skins by a quick dunk into boiling water—about 30 seconds. They may be coated with the honey-lemon solution or simply dried. Place on racks in the sun for several days, turning them every day. Cover or bring indoors at night. To make "dollar figs", stand them upright on the drying rack. After partly dry, push the top towards the rack to flatten it. When dry store in an air-tight container.

Fruit Leather

Fruit leather is easy to make and store. Choose any fruit desired. Over-ripe fruit may be used as long as bruised spots are removed. Cook into a puree, adding honey to taste. Spread on cookie sheets which have been lined with waxed paper. Cover with screens or cheesecloth and dry in the sun. When dry, cut the sheets into strips and roll up. Store in an air-tight container. Peel off the paper as you eat it.

Garlic

Garlic is ready to harvest when the tops fall over. Leaving the tops intact, pull the bulbs and leave them lying in the sun beside their rows. Leave them to dry for one day, then spread on racks in the shade where there is good air circulation. When tops have completely dried the garlic is ready to store. The tops may be braided and hung in a storage space or the bulbs can be packed in dry straw or newspaper.

Green Beans

Wash and cut beans into one-inch pieces. Spread on trays to dry in the sun. Drying is complete when beans are brittle in texture and greenish-black in color. They should be turned every day while drying.

Beans may also be dried whole. Use a large needle and heavy thread to string the beans, leaving about ½-inch of space between them. Hang in a warm attic or outside in the sun to dry.

Dried beans should be stored in air-tight containers. They are a delightful addition to soups or may be ground to be included in a vegetable powder. Use in combination with other dried vegetables for a soup base.

Lemon Peel

Finely grate the yellow of the peel. Spread it on a tray to dry in the sun or in a warm oven for a few hours. Store the dried peel in a jar for use in flavoring pies, cakes, or fish. Lemon peel is also a good addition to many blends of tea, both herb teas and black teas.

Lima Beans

Gather the lima beans while they are still green and in the pods. Shell the beans and spread on cheesecloth-covered trays in the sun. To stove-top dry, gather and prepare as above, steaming them for 8 to 10 minutes before spreading on trays to dry. They are completely dry when hard and wrinkled. Store in air-tight containers.

Mushrooms

Remove the stem from the button, but do not wash. String the button on a long cord, using a thin needle and being careful not to split the mushroom. Hang them in the sun to dry. Drying is complete when they are leathery and very dry. Store in air-tight glass jars.

To use, soak the mushrooms in warm water until soft and rinse several times to remove any dirt.

Onions

Onions are ready to harvest when the tops fall over. Pull the bulbs and lay them beside the rows in the sun. Leave for one day, then spread on racks in the shade where there is good air circulation. Leave to dry until the outer skin layer is paper dry. The tops may be braided and hung in a storage space or the bulbs can be packed in dry straw or newspaper. Always store in a cool, dry place.

For dried onion flakes, peel and shred or grate fresh onions. Spread on cheesecloth-lined trays and cover with a layer of cheesecloth so they don't blow away. The flakes will dry in one day in the full sun.

Parsley

Gather large curly parsley. Plunge each piece into boiling water; shake thoroughly. Bundle the pieces together and hang in a warm shaded area. When dry, crumble the parsley and discard the stems. Store in air-tight jars.

Peaches

Choose a freestone variety when it has just ripened. Wash, cut in half and remove pits. Treat for darkening with the honey-lemon mixture or the ascorbic acid dip. Spread cut side up in the sun. Cover or bring in each night. Allow 4 to 5 days to dry. When dry, peaches will have a leathery look and feel, with no moisture present when cut. Store in air-tight containers in a cool, dry place.

To stove-top or oven dry, prepare as above. Spread cut side down on a wire rack and dry at 120 to 150 degrees.

Pears

Firm, ripe Bartlett pears are best for drying. Peel, cut in half, and remove the core. Treat for darkening with the honey-lemon mixture or the ascorbic acid dip. Spread cut side up in the sun. Cover or bring in each night. Pears will take four to five days to dry. When dry, pears will be leathery-feeling and chewy. Store in an air-tight container in a cool, dry place. To stove-top or oven dry, prepare as above and dry at 120 to 150 degrees.

Peas

Peas may be dried in or out of the pods. To dry in the pods, harvest peas when just right for table use. Discard pods that are mildewed or spotted; do not wash. Spread on trays to dry in the sun. Peas are dry when you can hear them rattle in the pod when shaken. Shell and store in jars.

To stove-top or oven dry, shell fresh peas, discarding any yellowed ones. Steam blanch for 6 minutes. Spread on drying racks and dry at 120 degrees until hard and wrinkled.

Peppers

Small, hot peppers may be strung whole on heavy-weight bottom-hole thread, using a large needle. Larger peppers should be cut in half and seeded, then strung as above. Hang in a sunny, airy spot to dry. Peppers may also be dried in small pieces. To peel them, place under the broiler until the skins blister and get somewhat burnt-looking. Remove from broiler, allow to cool, and pull the skins off. Another way to remove the skins is to plunge whole peppers into boiling water for one minute, then into ice water. The skins will slip off. Remove the seeds and chop into small pieces. Spread in the hot sun to dry.

To stove-top or oven dry, proceed as above by removing the skins and chopping into small pieces. Drying at 120 degrees will take several hours. Store in air-tight jars.

Prunes

Prune plums are ready to dry when they fall from the tree. Do not remove the pits. Dip into boiling water for one or two minutes to destroy any insects. Spread on trays in the hot sun to dry. When dry, prunes should show no moisture but should have a chewy texture. Store in an air-tight container.

Raspberries

Remove the stems and spread in a single layer on drying trays. No moisture will be present when thoroughly dry. Store in air-tight containers.

To stove-top or oven dry, proceed as above and dry at 120 degrees.

Rhubarb

Wash and cut stalks into 1-inch pieces. String on heavy botton-hole thread with a large needle. Hang in a sunny, airy spot. When dry, no moisture should be present. Store in an air-tight container. Rhubarb can also be dried by placing on drying trays in the hot sun. Stripping off the outer skins aids in drying.

To stove-top or oven dry, preceed as above by placing on drying trays and dry at 120 degrees.

Soybeans

Soybeans are best dried in the garden. Leave them on the vines until the stalks, pods and leaves are completely dried and yellow-brown. If the rains come early, the plants may be pulled when mature and hung upside down in a warm, dry place. Shell as you would peas. Store in air-tight containers.

To stove-top or oven dry, harvest pods when ripe. Blanch the pods in steam for five minutes, then shell. Spread on drying trays and dry until hard and wrinkled.

Squash

All varieties of summer squash may be dried. Wash and cut into thin slices without peeling. Spread on drying racks. When dry, the squash will be hard and brittle. Store as dried or grind into powder for seasoning or soup base. May also be mixed with other dried vegetables to form a vegetable powder seasoning. To stove-top or oven dry, proceed as above and dry at 120 degrees.

Strawberries

Wash and stem the berries. Mix one part honey with three parts strawberries. Spread on drying racks in the hot sun. Stir or turn frequently. When dry, store in air-tight containers.

Tomatoes

Plunge the tomatoes into boiling water for one minute, then into cold water. Remove the skins when cool and chop into ½-inch pieces. Drain excess juice by placing tomatoes in a colander for several hours (save the juice for drinking or cooking). Spread chopped tomatoes on trays to dry. When dry, tomatoes will be brittle. Store in chunks or grind into powder for seasoning or soup base. May also be mixed with other dried vegetables to form a vegetable seasoning powder. To stove-top or oven dry, proceed as above.

Turnips

Wash turnips and cut them into thin slices. Spread on drying trays in the hot sun. When dry, turnips will be brittle. Store in glass jars or grind into a vegetable powder.

To stove-top or oven dry, slice very thin, then steam slices for 6 minutes. Allow to cool. Spread on trays and dry until brittle.

Appendix

Vegetables by Groups Vitamin Value	Pounds to Raise for Canning	Quarts to Can	Yield Per 100 ft. Row	Foot Row Needed	Seed or plants Per 100 ft. Row	Days to Maturity	Depth to Plant Seed	Distance Between Plants	Distance Between Rows
High in Vitamin A & C									
Spinach	40	20	50	90	1 oz.	40-50	½"	2-4"	12-18"
Turnip Greens	40	20	45	100	½ oz.	30	½"		
Broccoli	48	24	60	85	60 plants	80	½"	12-18"	30-36"
High in Vitamin A									
Carrots	40	20	75	60	½ oz.	55-75	½"	2-3"	12-18"
Sweet Potatoes	48	24	80	60	100 plants	120*		12-18"	36-48"
Winter Squash	40	20	400	10	½ oz. or 4-5 per hill	60-110	1"	9-12" 3' hills	84-120"
High in Vitamin C									
Tomato, whole	120	60	380	100	50 plants	50*	Not Staked	18-36"	36-60"
Tomato, juice	240	120							
Peppers	44	22	60	75	65 plants	70*		18-24"	18-24"
Cauliflower	72	36	120	60	60 plants	100*		18-24"	24-36"
Green Vegetables						*Days to maturity from plants, not from seed.			
Peas	48	24	40 pods	300	1 lb.	50-60	2"	2"	18-24"
Green Beans	120	60	60	200	1 lb.	40-60	1-2"	4"	18-24"
Okra	30	15	65	55	1 oz.		1"	12"	36"
Starchy Vegetables									
Sweet Corn	72	36	85 ears	200	4 oz.	60-90	1-2"	9-12"	24-48"
Lima Beans	48	24	25 pods	400	12 oz.	60-75	1-2"	8-10"	18-30"
Vegetables for Variety									
Beets	24	12	60	40	1 oz.	50-70	½-1"	2-4"	12-18"
Cucumbers			100	20	½ oz. 4-5 per hill		½-1"	12" 3' hills	40-72"
Lettuce Leaf				15			½"	8"	18-24"
Onions			100	10	2 lbs. sets				12-18"
Radish			100	10		25-30	½"	1-2"	12-18"
Turnips	24	12	100	25	½ oz.	50-60	½"	6"	12-18"
Pumpkin	24	12	300	10	½ oz. 4-5 per hill	90-100	1"	24" 3' hills	84-120"

Buying Calendar for Fresh Fruits and Vegetables

MONTH	FRUITS		VEGETABLES	
January	Apples Avocados Grapefruit Lemons	Navel oranges Tangerines Winter pears	Beets Cabbage Cauliflower Celery	Lettuce Potatoes Spinach
February	Apples Avocados Grapefruit Lemons	Navel oranges Tangerines Winter pears	Artichokes Beets Broccoli Cabbage Cauliflower	Celery Lettuce Potatoes Spinach
March	Apples Avocados Grapefruit	Lemons Navel oranges Winter pears	Artichokes Asparagus Beets Broccoli Cabbage	Carrots Cauliflower Celery Potatoes Spinach
April	Apples Avocados Grapefruit Lemons	Navel oranges Strawberries Winter pears	Artichokes Asparagus Beets Broccoli Carrots	Cauliflower Lettuce Peas Spinach
May	Avocados Cherries Grapefruit Lemons	Navel oranges Valencia oranges Strawberries	Asparagus Beets Cabbage Carrots Celery Lettuce	Onions Peas Potatoes Spinach Sweet corn Tomatoes
June	Apricots Avocados Bushberries Cantaloupe Cherries Figs Honey dew melon	Lemons Nectarines Peaches Plums Strawberries Valencia oranges Watermelon	Carrots Celery Cucumbers Green (snap) beans Lettuce Tomatoes	Onions Peppers Potatoes Summer squash Sweet corn

July	Apricots	Nectarines	Cabbage	Lettuce
	Avocados	Peaches	Carrots	Okra
	Bushberries	Pears	Celery	Onions
	Cantaloupe	Plums	Cucumbers	Peppers
	Grapefruit	Strawberries	Eggplant	Potatoes
	Honey dew melon	Valencia oranges	Green (snap) beans	Summer squash
	Lemons	Watermelon	Green lima beans	Sweet corn
			Tomatoes	
August	Avocados	Nectarines	Cabbage	Okra
	Cantaloupe	Peaches	Celery	Onions
	Figs	Pears	Cucumbers	Peppers
	Grapes	Persian melon	Eggplant	Potatoes
	Grapefruit	Valencia oranges	Green (snap) beans	Summer squash
	Honey dew melon	Watermelon	Green lima beans	Sweet corn
	Lemons		Lettuce	Tomatoes
September	Apples	Lemons	Cabbage	Onions
	Cantaloupe	Peaches	Cucumbers	Peas
	Figs	Pears	Eggplant	Peppers
	Grapes	Persian melon	Green (snap) beans	Summer squash
	Grapefruit	Plums and prunes	Green lima beans	Sweet corn
	Honey dew melon	Valencia oranges	Lettuce	Tomatoes
October	Apples	Pears	Broccoli	Okra
	Dates	Persian melon	Brussels sprouts	Peas
	Figs	Persimmons	Cabbage	Peppers
	Grapes	Valencia oranges	Carrots	Potatoes
	Lemons		Cucumbers	Sweet corn
			Eggplant	Sweet potatoes
			Green (snap) beans	Tomatoes
			Green lima beans	Winter squash
			Lettuce	
November	Almonds	Grapes	Broccoli	Lettuce
	Apples	Lemons	Brussels sprouts	Peas
	Avocados	Persimmons	Cabbage	Peppers
	Dates	Walnuts	Carrots	Potatoes
			Cauliflower	Sweet corn
			Celery	Sweet potatoes
			Eggplant	Winter squash
			Green (snap) beans	
December	Almonds	Grapefruit	Broccoli	Celery
	Apples	Lemons	Brussels sprouts	Spinach
	Avocados	Navel oranges	Carrots	Sweet potatoes
	Dates	Walnuts	Cauliflower	Winter squash

Canning Problems

Jars do not seal because:

— the jar was filled too full and the lid did not close properly.
— the jar rim was chipped or the rim was not adequately wiped off after filling. Particles of food came between the sealing compound and the rim of the jar.
— jar lids were not used according to the manufacturer's directions. The lids were either too hot or too cold for a good seal.
— a scratch across the sealing compound left an air space that prevented a complete seal.
— screw band was bent or rusty and did not hold lid firmly against the rim of jar.
— screw band was tightened after jar was removed from the canner.

Foods spoil because:

— no altitude correction was made at elevations above 2,000 feet.
— water-bath was not kept at a full boil throughout the entire processing time.
— water level in the canner dropped below the tops of the jars.

Foods change color because:

— foods were too long in preparation.
— food was not processed long enough to destroy the enzymes that affect color.
— foods were over-processed.
— liquid in the jars did not completely cover the food. Exposed portions became discolored.
— air bubbles were not removed.
— fruits such as apples and pears were not treated with ascorbic acid to keep color.
— high color in foods such as beets or cherries dissolved in the liquid or syrup.
— food was stored in too warm a place or where the light was exceptionally strong.

Foods float because:

— food was packed too loosely in the jar.
— syrup was too heavy for the fruit.
— raw-pack products tend to float more than those that have some pre-cooking. More air remains in the tissues of uncooked food at the time it goes in the jar.
— food was processed too long.
— fruit was too ripe.

Sediment collects in bottom of jars because:

— minerals present in the water used for precooking foods or for filling the jars settled out.
— table salt with an anti-caking ingredient was used in place of pure sea salt or pickling salt.
— fruits were overripe.

Liquid is lost or low because:

— food was packed too tightly or jars were too full. The product boiled over and started a siphoning action.
— air bubbles were not removed.
— water was less than one inch over the tops of the jars in a water-bath canner.

Equivalent Temperatures
Celsius and Fahrenheit

°C	= °F		°C	= °F		°C	= °F
150	302		85	185		20	68
145	293		80	176		15	59
140	284		75	167		10	50
135	275		70	158		5	41
130	266		65	149		0	32
125	257		60	140		-5	23
120	248		55	131		-10	14
115	239		50	122		-15	5
110	230		45	113		-20	-4
105	221		40	104		-25	-13
100	212		35	95		-30	-22
95	203		30	86		-35	-31
90	194		25	77		-40	-40

To convert Fahrenheit into Celsius (Centigrade), subtract 32, multiply by 5, divide by 9. $°F - 32 \times 5 \div 9 = °C$

To convert Celsius into Fahrenheit, reverse the formula: multiply by 9, divide by 5, add 32. $°C \times 9 \div 5 + 32 = °F$

Index

photo by linda sanchez

ABOUT THE AUTHOR:

Susan Geiskopf was born in Honolulu, January 1950. She spent her early school days with her family in England and moved to California in the early 60's. She has a degree in psychology from California State University, Sacramento, has taught kindergarten, and has been a designer and manufacturer of jewelry. She is currently a hat designer and operates a boutique in Sacramento. Susan became interested in canning years ago when the garden overflowed. Unable to find many recipes using honey, her canning became a systematic, experimental project to develop honey recipes and techniques which evolved into **Putting it Up with Honey.**